UFU's

NAZI
SECRET
WEAPON?

MATTERN·FRIEDRICH

SAMISDAT PUBLISHERS LTD.
Toronto, Canada

Printed in Canada

DEDICATION

This book is dedicated by the authors, their collaborators and the publishers to the unsung and often-maligned heroes of the Second World War.

Mattern

Every effort has been made by the authors to give credit to the originators of material whether it be written or pictorial. However, the search for such originators sometimes proved fruitless. Should anyone not be included, it is solely due to the confusing maze of claims and counterclaims to copyrights.

FORWORD

Ever since the fall of Berlin and the unconditional surrender of the German armed forces in 1945 one continually reads of Adolf Hitler's possible or definite escape from Berlin and Germany. Hitler has been reported to be living in several inaccessible spots in South America, in some well-guarded Shang-ri-la surrounded by S.S. Guards armed to the teeth. He is supposed to have spent some time in a monastery in Spain and other reports have him as a "prisoner" in Russia, itself.

Millions of words have been written and spoken to this effect. Over 100,000 books have been written about Hitler and W.W. II in most major languages of the world. Most of them were more or less fictional accounts and re-hashes of the official propaganda lines and clichés of the military victors of W.W. II. None of these studies were deep or exhaustive enough to be considered conclusive. Many very important facets were not covered at all or were only touched upon the fringes.

The book that is before you, is to the knowledge of the authors, their collaborators and to the publishers as well, the first attempt to cover some of these fringe issues in more depth. Consequently, they have drawn some very different conclusions to those already written on this vast and complex topic.

In order to start on a sound footing, and ultimately to do it justice, Hitler, the man is examined. Hitler, the thinker, the statesman, the politician and above all, Hitler the founder of the National Socialist Ideology (Weltanschauung) is examined in greater detail and in a more dispassionate manner. To only write about the technical aspects and ratifications of the UFO mystery, of the UFO's purely military potential, would, of necessity, lead to incorrect conclusions.

To separate the totality of Hitler's control and influence over the production and eventual use of the UFO's and over every other secret development of the II Reich would be stupid. Without Hitler's backing or his knowledge of their potential uses, no weapons, not even the UFO's would have been developed; they would have been condemned to the "planners' morgue" or the junk piles.

Hitler knew about the research work being done on UFO's by his scientists, just as he knew about the other incredible secret weapons they were feverishly working upon in their bomb-proof laboratories. Many of these highly sophisticated

3

weapon systems represented scientific breakthroughs of great importance. Many of these devices fell into Allied hands and they are pictured here for the first time and to the best of our knowledge. Others are re-created from engineering drawings or from testimony given to the Allied interrogators.

There is a whole array of jet and rocket-powered aircraft, both fighters and bombers. There are T.V. guided missiles and torpedos. There are plane and submarine-based rockets. Also there are wind cannons and many other devices.

In order to understand all aspects of this vexing problem we have to examine the governmental set-up of National Socialist Germany, especially war-time Germany. Unlike any other state in recorded history, Hitler's Germany was literally run by one man, much in the shape of a pyramid, with the chain of command moving down and out. In Hitler's hands ended all the strands; from his pinnacle of absolute power emanated all orders. From Hitler came the final orders of the scrapping or the production of any kind of weaponry. He alone was capable of making available the vast amounts of money for the research and production of what was needed to win the war. He alone could delegate the sweeping powers and set the orders of priority of one weapon system over any other.

All attempts to clarify this or that aspect of the German war effort, of diplomatic or military moves, which do not take fully into account this pyramidical structure of the decision-making process in Nazi Germany, are doomed to dismal failure. This structure of National Socialism is the very foundation of the movement, it is the "Führerprinzip" — leadership principle — in action. It is the failure or deliberate unwillingness to understand this basic principle, that has been the undoing of 95% of the writers, historians and media people of the world. By ignoring this simple principle in action and its effect on all things the origins of the UFO's (Krautmeteors), their current whereabouts and status, as well as Hitler's fate, have been shrouded in mystery and often contradictions.

The author of this book and his friends started to delve into the UFO mystery. They circulated their findings over the years to an ever-increasing number of friends and contacts around the world, but only as a basis for discussion and further study. Whenever more reports of UFO crews speaking German (Kearny Report) and behaving like German soldiers (electricity blackout Eastern States), or of sightings and documentation (French T.V. showed a UFO landing gear imprint in

4

a clear swastika shape), reached the authors, they took a closer look. There now appeared a distinguishable pattern, in proper time and date sequence, that hinted at a possible connection between the appearance of UFO's in large numbers and Hitler's possible survival and escape from Berlin.

A book was born. Many publishers were contacted, all thought the material had merit, but none dared to publish it in its entirety. Many wanted to publish only the UFO developments. All would have loved to reproduce the hither-to unpublished engineering drawings and illustrations of prototypes of the German UFO's and the many other secret weapons but the authors insisted it was to be all or nothing.

So the manuscript made the rounds for years and years. Eventually it lay buried. Then one day, excerpts fell into the hands of a group of individuals who decided to collect money amongst themselves and publish the manuscript. With the help and active participation of the authors and their collaborators the book is now before you.

Against threats and persecution this courageous group of individuals composed of diverse ethnic backgrounds, has stood firm. We ask of the reader only to reserve judgement until he has thoroughly read through the book to the very last page. This book is not an easy book to read. One could almost call it an unnerving study of a very unusual and extraordinary man, his ideas his actions, his motivations and his ultimate goals. It also gives one a glimpse of German inventiveness and their capacity to suffer punishment and to be able to rise Phoenix-like from the ashes of "total defeat". This book also shows Hitler's opponents in a new light; in the light of truth and not propaganda. The book can further serve the unprejudiced individual as a catalyst to study and re-examine many events from a new perspective. Now that many Allied documents are being de-classified, a new search will produce new and startling insights and conclusions.

We believe that the open-minded reader after studying this book and after delving into the many reference and source materials listed, will never again look at the world with the same eyes.

The publishers

P.S. Those of you fortunate enough to be able to speak and to read German will find a considerable difference between the English and German editions. The reasons are simply:

1. Difficulty in finding translators for such a deeply philosophical work.

2. The English-speaking readership is used to material in this lighter vein.

For the above reasons, this is not a true translation of the German version but rather a book about another book.

Hitler planning

THE MIND AND PERSONALITY OF ADOLF HITLER

The non-German world has a rather sketchy and fragmentary picture of the mind of Adolf Hitler; how he thought, felt and what motivated him. Lacking accurate knowledge, no one can possibly claim to understand the personality of this extraordinary man. Consequently, we will try to condense into a few paragraphs, what has taken historians volumes and volumes of books to describe.

Adolf Hitler was, above all else, an intuitive, artistic human being, capable of accurately sensing situations and of grasping them with the clarity of an extremely orderly mind. He believed in the absolute supremacy of the spirit over the material, and this was borne out by his now-famous statement that for him, and for a National Socialist, two words did not exist in the dictionary — **impossible** (unmoglich) and **never** (niemals).

Let us look at his own life as a case in point. An early orphan, poor, with incomplete education, a stateless citizen in Germany with a sickly physical constitution, and, after the First World War, penniless and without a job or trade. He was just one of the many millions of Germans in similar desperate straits at that time in history. He had, one has to admit, not a chance to be anything other, even if lucky, than a manual labourer. Impossible, one would have to concede, that this man could ever become Mayor of Munich let alone the Chancellor of the largest, most populous, best-trained and educated country in the heart of Europe. Never — not in his circumstances!

Impossible? Never? Well, the entire world is witness to the fact that not only did the impossible become possible, it actually happened and in a very short period of time. The **never** and **impossible** were stricken from his and from history's dictionary.

Here enters the very first and most important component in understanding Adolf Hitler, and through it, the partial solution to the U.F.O. riddle.

Nothing in National Socialism was ever allowed to seem an impossible task or an unattainable goal. With Adolf Hitler it was always mind over matter. The belief then held by aircraft designers that the human body could not survive space flight and faster-than-sound speeds was scornfully put on one side by Hitler and it was his challenging of this belief that brought forth the U.F.O.'s.

Let us now return to the other facets of Hitler's mind in order to get an even clearer picture.

Hitler felt, based on his studies and an enormous amount of reading, that there existed a very definite plan by a small, but immensely powerful group of Jewish bankers, financiers, industrialists and others, to take control of the entire world. It is important to remember that he lived in Vienna during a time when a very noisy battle was raging between Zionist Jews, (who wanted to be a separate race, religion, nation and culture with their own state, Israel), and the assimilated elements amongst the Jews, (who wanted to be part of the cosmopolitan establishment of the Austrian Empire), with all the privileges and power their immense wealth bestowed on them. Hitler's appraisal of the Jews can best be summed up as contained in "The Protocols of the Learned Elders of Zion". This is a very important aspect of the whole U.F.O. story, because in it, we find the seeds for many far-reaching decisions made 30 years later. Hitler saw in this actual or imagined Jewish drive for world domination, a very definite danger to his own work and plan.

From now on we must look at every problem from this vantage point. Hitler would undoubtedly double-check each major question by this criterion: "How would I act in this case if I were a Jew bent on world conquest?" Now we have the two most important keys to understanding the functioning of his mind.

There is, however, another very important fact, and this is motivation. What motivated this man? Why should this penniless and jobless vagrant, (often disparagingly called a paperhanger) act the way he did? Millions of words have been devoted to this question. All, or most of them, completely misrepresented him, and this is especially true in the non-German world where he is portrayed as some power-mad maniac, seeking power solely for destructive reasons. This kind of thinking might have been justifiable as propaganda during war time, but the truth requires a long over-due re-evaluation, and the truth is simple.

The artistic, sensitive soul in this man rebelled at what he saw taking place around him. Since no single person, no group, no party and no ideology at that time expressed his feelings, he started expressing his own frustrations and ideas at the meetings of others. To his complete amazement he found that others listened and they listened in ever-increasing numbers. Thus, Hitler the agitator, the motivator, was born. There is no motivator without motivation and it was the concept of National Socialism that was his motivation.

It is neither the intent nor the desire of the authors to re-write "Mein Kampf" and we shall restrict ourselves to the very barest of outlines to clarify his motivations. This is necessary to solve the U.F.O. riddle and can best be summed up in the 24 points of the N.S.D.A.P. Party Programme and also are reflected in a study Hitler made of the political situation for the army in Munich, where he was "Political Information Officer".

THE PROGRAMME OF THE PARTY

THE Programme of the German Workers' Party is limited as to period. The leaders have no intention, once the aims announced in it have been achieved, of setting up fresh ones, in order to ensure the continued existence of the Party by the artificially increased discontent of the masses.

1. We demand the union of all Germans, on the basis of the right of the self-determination of peoples, to form a Great Germany.

2. We demand equality of rights for the German People in its dealings with other nations, and abolition of the Peace Treaties of Versailles and St. Germain.

3. We demand land and territory (colonies) for the nourishment of our people and for settling our surplus population.

4. None but members of the nation may be citizens of the State. None but those of German blood, whatever their creed, may be members of the nation. No Jew, therefore, may be a member of the nation.

5. Anyone who is not a citizen of the State may live in Germany only as a guest and must be regarded as being subject to the Alien laws.

6. The right of voting on the leadership and legislation is to be enjoyed by the citizens of the State alone.

We demand, therefore, that all official appointments, of whatever kind, whether in the Reich, the provinces, or the small communities, shall be granted to citizens of the State alone.

We oppose the corrupt Parliamentary custom of the State of filling posts merely with a view to Party considerations, and without reference to character or capacity.

7. We demand that the State shall make it its first duty to promote the industry and livelihood of the citizens of the State. If it is not possible to nourish the entire population of the State, foreign nationals (non-citizens of the State) must be excluded from the Reich.

8. All further non-German immigration must be prevented. We demand that all non-Germans who entered Germany subsequently to August 2, 1914, shall be required forthwith to depart from the Reich.

9. All citizens of the State shall possess equal rights and duties.

10. It must be the first duty of every citizen of the State to perform mental or physical work. The activities of the individual must not clash with the interests of the whole, but must proceed within the framework of the community and must be for the general good.

We demand therefore:

11. Abolition of incomes unearned by work. Abolition of the thraldom of interest.

12. In view of the enormous sacrifice of life and property demanded of a nation by every war, personal enrichment through war must be regarded as a crime against the nation. We demand therefore the ruthless confiscation of all war profits.

13. We demand the nationalization of all businesses which have (hitherto) been amalgamated (into Trusts).

14. We demand that there shall be profit-sharing in the great industries.

15. We demand a generous development of provision for old age.

16. We demand the creation and maintenance of a healthy middle class, immediate communalization of wholesale warehouses, and their lease at a low rate to small traders, and that the most careful consideration shall be shown to all small purveyors to the State, the provinces, or smaller communities.

17. We demand a land-reform suitable to our national requirements, the passing of a law for the confiscation without compensation of land for communal purposes, the abolition of interest on mortgages, and prohibition of all speculation in land.

On 13 April 1928, Adolf Hitler made the following declaration:

"It is necessary to reply to the false interpretation on the part of our opponents of Point 17 of the Programme of the NSDAP.

"Since the NSDAP admits the principle of private property, it is obvious that the expression 'confiscation without compensation' refers merely to the creation of possible legal means of confiscating, when necessary, land illegally acquired, or not administered in accordance with the national welfare. It is therefore directed in the first instance against the Jewish companies which speculate in land."

"(Signed) ADOLF HITLER."

"Munich, April 13, 1928."

18. We demand ruthless war upon all those whose activities are injurious to the common interest. Common criminals against the nation, usurers, profiteers, &c., must be punished with death, whatever their creed or race.

19. We demand that the Roman Law, which serves the materialistic world order, shall be replaced by a German common law.

20. With the aim of opening to every capable and industrious German the possibility of higher education and consequent advancement to leading positions the State must consider a thorough reconstruction of our national system of education. The curriculum of all educational establishments must be brought into line with the requirements of practical life. Directly the mind begins to develop the schools must aim at teaching the pupil to understand the idea of the State (State sociology). We demand the education of specially gifted children of poor parents, whatever their class or occupation, at the expense of the State.

21. The State must apply itself to raising the standard of health in the nation by protecting mothers and infants,

prohibiting child labour, and increasing bodily efficiency by legally obligatory gymnastics and sports, and by extensive support of clubs engaged in the physical training of the young.

22. We demand the abolition of mercenary troops and the formation of a national army.

23. We demand legal warfare against conscious political lies and their dissemination in the Press. In order to facilitate the creation of a German national Press we demand:

(*a*) that all editors and contributors to newspapers employing the German language must be members of the nation;

(*b*) That special permission from the State shall be necessary before non-German newspapers may appear. These need not necessarily be printed in the German language;

(*c*) That non-Germans shall be prohibited by law from participating financially in or influencing German newspapers, and that the penalty for contravention of the law shall be suppression of any such newspaper, and immediate deportation of the non-German involved.

It must be forbidden to publish newspapers which do not conduce to the national welfare. We demand the legal prosecution of all tendencies in art and literature of a kind likely to disintegrate our life as a nation, and the suppression of institutions which militate against the above-mentioned requirements.

24. We demand liberty for all religious denominations in the State, so far as they are not a danger to it and do not militate against the morality and moral sense of the German race.

The Party, as such, stands for positive Christianity, but does not bind itself in the matter of creed to any particular confession. It combats the Jewish-materialist spirit *within* and *without* us, and is convinced that our nation can achieve permanent health from within only on the principle: the common interest before self-interest.

25. That all the foregoing requirements may be realized we demand the creation of a strong central power of the Reich. Unconditional authority of the politically central Parliament over the entire Reich and its organization in general.

The formation of Diets and vocational Chambers for the purpose of executing the general laws promulgated by the Reich in the various States of the Confederation.

The leaders of the Party swear to proceed regardless of consequences—if necessary at the sacrifice of their lives—towards the fulfilment of the foregoing Points.[1]

MUNICH, February 24, 1920.

In a meeting held in the Circus Krone on 18 September 1922 Hitler formulated "some fundamental demands of the Party":

"1. We must call to account the November criminals of 1918. It cannot be that two million Germans should have fallen in vain and that afterwards one should sit down as friends at the same table with traitors. No, we do not pardon, we demand—Vengeance!"

"2. The dishonouring of the nation must cease. For betrayers of their Fatherland and informers the gallows is the proper place. Our streets and squares shall once more bear the names of our heroes; they shall not be named after Jews. In the Question of Guilt we must proclaim the truth".

"3. The administration of the State must be cleared of the rabble which is fattened at the stall of the parties".

"4. The present laxity in the fight against usury must be abandoned. Here the fitting punishment is the same as that for the betrayers of their Fatherland".

"5. We must demand a great enlightenment on the subject of the Peace Treaty. With thoughts of love? No! but in holy hatred against those who have ruined us".

"6. The lies which would veil from us our misfortunes must cease. The fraud of the present money-madness must be shown up. That will stiffen the necks of us all".

"7. As foundation for a new currency the property of those who are not of our blood must do service. If families who have lived in Germany for a thousand years are now expropriated, we must do the same to the Jewish usurers".

"8. We demand immediate expulsion of all Jews who have entered Germany since 1914, and of all those, too, who through trickery on the Stock Exchange or through other shady transactions have gained their wealth".

"9. The housing scarcity must be relieved through energetic action; houses must be granted to those who deserve them. Eisner said in 1918 that we had no right to demand the return of our prisoners—he was only saying openly what all Jews were thinking. People who so think must feel how life tastes in a concentration camp!"

"Extremes must be fought by extremes. Against the infection of materialism, against the Jewish pestilence we must hold aloft a flaming ideal. And if others speak of the World and Humanity we say The Fatherland—and only the Fatherland!"[1]

Hitler's "Study of the Jews" — for the army

In so far as the danger with which Jewry threatens our people today finds its expression in an undeniable aversion experienced by the majority of our people, the cause of that aversion is not generally to be found in a clear awareness of the Jews' systematically destructive effect, whether conscious or unconscious, on our nation as a whole, but arises mainly from personal intercourse and the impression made by the Jew as an individual. . . . Thus antisemitism all too easily takes on the character of a mere manifestation of emotion. And that is wrong. As a political movement antisemitism cannot and must not be determined by emotional motives but by a recognition of the facts . . . : To begin with, Jewry is incontestably a race and not a religious community. And the Jew himself never describes himself as a Jewish German, Jewish Pole or, say, a Jewish American, but always as a German, Polish or American Jew. In no case has the Jew ever . . . assimilated very much more from other nations than their language. . . . Even the Mosaic faith . . . is not the final word on the question of Jew or non-Jew. . . . By a thousand years of inbreeding, often occurring within a very small circle, the Jew has generally kept his race and type more sharply defined than the peoples among whom he lives. The result of this is that we have in our midst a non-German, foreign race neither willing nor able to sacrifice its racial characteristics or to renounce its own way of feeling, thinking and striving and which nevertheless has just the same political rights as us. If the Jew's very feelings are concerned with the purely material, how much more so his thinking and striving. The dance round the Golden Calf becomes a merciless struggle for all those possessions which to our way of feeling ought not to be the only and ultimate things worth striving for. The value of an individual is no longer determined by his character, by the importance of his achievements to the whole, but exclusively by the size of his fortune. . . . A nation's stature is no longer to be reckoned by the sum of its moral and spiritual forces but only by the profusion of its worldly goods. From this feeling there arises that thinking, that striving after money and after the power to protect it, which leads the Jew to be unscrupulous in his choice of methods, and pitiless in applying them. . . . In an autocratically governed State he whines to gain the 'majesty's', the prince's, favour which he abuses [by battening] on his subjects like a leach. In a democracy he goes whoring after the favour of the masses, crawls before the 'majesty of the people' and knows only the majesty of money. He destroys the prince's character by Byzantine flattery, and national pride – the strength of a people – by mockery and the shameless promotion of vice. His weapon is public opinion . . . which he guides and distorts by means of the Press. His power is the power of money which in his hands proliferates unceasingly and effortlessly in the form of interest. . . . Everything that induces men to aspire to higher things, be it religion, socialism, or democracy, is to him only a means to an end – that of satisfying his lust for money and domination. He acts on the peoples like racial tuberculosis. And as a consequence anti-semitism arising out of purely emotional reasons will find its ultimate expression in the form of progroms [sic]. Antisemitism based on reason, however, must lead to a systematic and legal campaign to deprive the Jew of the privileges which he alone of all the foreigners in our midst enjoys (Aliens Legislation). But its final goal must always remain the removal of the Jews as a whole.

It could be said that we are a little far off the U.F.O. problem but without this groundwork it is not possible to unravel this very complex story. We now have a clear picture of the basic working of Hitler's brain. We know how he felt about "his enemies", real or imagined, and we also know what motivated him in his political moves and decisions.

To sum up:—

1. Hitler never thought anything impossible; he never accepted defeat. Hitler did not believe that even death was the end and thought of death only as a transition, after which the struggle continued only on a different plane. This can be clearly seen in his words "Und Ihr habt doch gesiegt" — "And you were victorious in spite of death" — often repeated during memorial speeches while honouring those of his supporters who fell during the march on the Feld-herrnhalle on November 23rd, 1923 in Munich. This same thinking permeates his last two public speeches broadcast January 10th, 1945 and February 25th, 1945 in which he re-affirmed that Germany would still win the war — ". . . and the Last Battalion will be ours".

2. Hitler saw a world-wide conspiracy of Jews and their Allies, (democrats, liberals, social democrats and marxists) in a concerted, well-planned drive for Jewish world domina-

tion. He argued vehemently and convincingly to untold millions of Europeans that there was a struggle taking place for a Jewish world in which all non-Jews were to be mere work slaves, with Jewish rulers, similar to those forming the Communist government in the Soviet Union, e.g., Trotsky (Bronstein), Litvinoff (Finkelstein), Kanganovich (Cohen), Ehrenburg and Berija, or for an Aryan world where the white man played a forceful dynamic role in global affairs, based on self-determination but within strict limits of a larger white world or what the Germans call "Abendland".

3. Hitler's motivating force was an unusual synthesis, (never before or since attempted), of the best features of **Socialism** and of **Free Enterprise** as opposed to multi-national corporations, (then called monopoly or state capitalism) on the one side, and Nationalism (based on ethnic origin and adherence) versus universalism or internationalism on the other. Hitler's synthesis worked and it was eminently successful all over Europe, providing full employment, financial stability (zero inflation) and introducing the greatest worker-benefit programmes of any modern, industrial state. It was never defeated as an idea but only destroyed (by military power), as a system.

An idea can only be superseded or defeated by another, better idea. Germany was only defeated militarily in 1945 but the idea of National Socialism is still as strong as ever and is flourishing around the world, but by necessity, underground.

The above three factors must constantly be kept in mind as we move from chapter to chapter and from event to event in the following pages.

SCIENTIFIC RESEARCH ESPECIALLY IN THE AIRCRAFT FIELD IN N.S. Germany

When Germany sent unmanned guided missiles, in the form of the V.1 and later the V.2 (the V standing for Vergeltungswaffen or Revenge Weapon), crashing into England as payment for England's treason against Europe, a weapon was thus introduced to the astonished world that up to that time had only been written about in Science Fiction magazines.

Again, the "impossible" had been realised. There was no defence in England against the V.2 and there would have been no defence against the A.9 and A.10 (America Rockets) which were destined to rain on New York and Washington in the Fall of 1945. These rockets were intended as revenge for the aimless and merciless killing of German civilians by the saturation fire-bombing of German cities by the U.S. Air Terrorists.

The breakthrough in the rocket weapon field by Germany so astonished the Allied leadership that Winston Churchill, fearing panic would break out in England,, contemplated germ warfare against Germany. It was only a lack of germs that prevented such action. However, the rocket breakthrough came too late to turn the tide for Germany. Conventional mass-bombing and mass-killing by the Allies took such a heavy toll that the war ended before all the new technology developed by German genius could be brought into the war. It was the knowledge that it was quantity winning over quality that had driven the hopelessly outnumbered German soldiers to despair, and the new technology gave them a feeling of relief plus the knowledge that only for a space of time had mass overwhelmed spirit.

Secret Weapons

General Eisenhower wrote in his book "Crusade in Europe": "It seems likely that if the Germans had succeeded in perfecting and using these new weapons six months earlier than they did, our invasion of Europe would have proved exceedingly difficult, perhaps impossible. I feel sure that had they succeeded in using these weapons over a six month period, particularly if he (Hitler) had made the Portsmouth-Southampton (landing) area one of his principle targets, Overlord (the invasion) might have been written off". Those were the "conventional" V. I and V. II rockets mentioned by Eisenhower with such awe.

Winston Churchill spoke of the "miracle weapons" that Goebbels had promised the Germans, and that if they had come half a year earlier Hitler would have driven the allies out of Europe!

It is interesting to speculate about what weapons these two allied war leaders were referring to. Some were undoubtedly the remote controlled missiles, V.I and V.II already mentioned. But there were others. There were ground-to-air missiles, some radio-controlled, some heat-seeking, some radar-guided and others even more sophisticated.

17

Long Range Rockets (ICBM) The "Amerika Rocket" at extreme left was to be operational by Fall-Winter 1945. (Note size of man in relation to size of rockets). Some of the German jet planes on the drawing boards and in the test stage. The experienced observer can trace most "modern developments" to these ancestors. Germany was at least a generation ahead of the rest of the world in "conventional" aircraft design

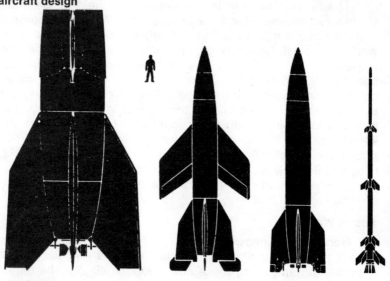

Abb. 217-220. **Fernraketen.** Von links nach rechts: A-9/A-10; A-4b und A-4 (V 2) von Peenemünde; ganz rechts: Rheinmetall „Rheinbote".

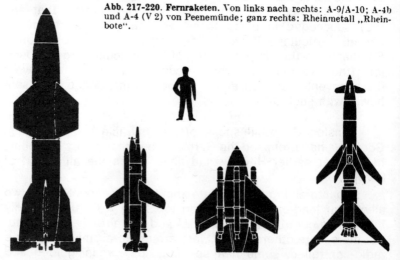

Abb. 221-224. **Fla-Raketen.** Von links nach rechts: Peenemünde C-2 „Wasserfall"; Henschel Hs 117 „Schmetterling"; Konrad „Enzian E-1"; Rheinmetall „Rheintochter R. 1"

18

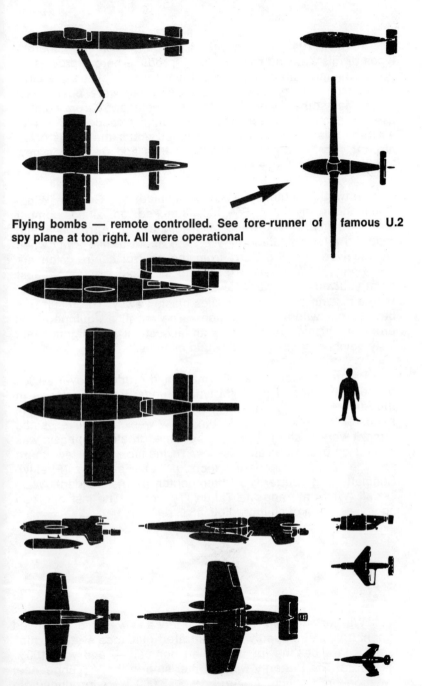

Flying bombs — remote controlled. See fore-runner of famous U.2 spy plane at top right. All were operational

Abb. 225-231. Fliegende Bomben. Oben links: Blohm & Voss BV 143; oben rechts: BV 246 B; mitte: Fieseler Fi 103 (V 1); unten links: Henschel Hs 293 A-O; unten mitte: Hs 294; untere Reihe rechts oben: Hs 298; untere Reihe rechts unten: Kramer X-4.

In April 1945, Germany had, in fact, over 130 different types of missiles and rockets. We reproduce here a cross-section of the most important types. Please note their size relative to the size of a man. All the ones pictured were operational types. Many others were just days or weeks away from combat use. Amongst them were the devastatingly successful R.4-M, air-to-air missiles which were mounted under the wings of an aircraft. A ME-110 could carry 48 R.4M's and Germany's new jets carried 24 of these murderously effective weapons.

Luftwaffe Lieutenant Werner Schneider, a German Wing-Commander, flying a F.W.190, attacked on allied bomber formation near the town of Schweinfurth in April 1945 and reported after his landing, "We were about a mile away when we received our directions from the control centre. 'You are close enough' a missile expert told us. 'Hold that range. Just point your noses forward towards them and pull the switches.' With a hissing sound the missiles blasted away. The result was beyond our wildest expectations. The missiles equipped with proximity fuses, some also with acoustical detonators, sent forty bombers to the ground within minutes."

Before the war ended, Germany had produced over 20,000 of these missiles of the R4M type in underground factories in the Sudetenland. Allied sources have put bomber losses at the hands of the R4M to over 500 in a few weeks. However, since aircraft were in short supply at that time, greater emphasis was placed on ground to air missiles. To mention but a few, there are the Enzian (Gentian), Hecht (Pike), Feuerlilie (Firelily), Schmetterling (Butterfly), Rheintochter (Rhine maiden), Wasserfall (Waterfall) and the Taifun (Typhoon). The last one had an acceleration of an incredible 45 G's.

Wasserfall could reach 50,000 feet and was later improved upon. It was equipped with an infrared guidance system which sent it in a beeline for any Allied bomber — and was 100% accurate. The Butterfly was another step in the V (Vengeance) weapon programme. In April 1945, 3,000 were produced; in June it was to be 10,000 missiles of this type alone.

When V.E. day came around, on May 8th, 1945, many expert analysts amongst the victors expressed the opinion that not a single allied plane would have been able to penetrate the borders of the German Reich after May, 1945. Germany's defence curtain of anti-aircraft missiles would have been 100% fool proof. Not even the atomic bomb would have been able to be "delivered", not to mention the fact that London and Washington were by that time within range of existing Germany long-range rockets and jet bombers. But there are other weapons to be mentioned here.

There was the "Lafferenz Projects" which was just completed at the time it permitted the firing of missiles from submerged U-Boats. Attacks were planned on cities such as New York, Boston, Philadelphia, Washington and even far-off Detroit.

Tests had been completed using small-scale subs and rockets (Lake Topliz, Austria) and large V.II's towed behind a submarine off Cuxhaven on the North Sea. Then there were flying bombs with built-in computer-controlled T.V. cameras, controlled by pilots who could be hundreds of miles away. There were long-range jet bombers, with 12,000 mile range, jet aircraft — aircraft carriers, transport planes that carried other smaller planes (12 of them) piggyback to their target area and then let loose their cargo of death and destruction. There were ram jets, jet fighters, bombers, transports and there was even an SST transport capable of flying four times the speed of sound.

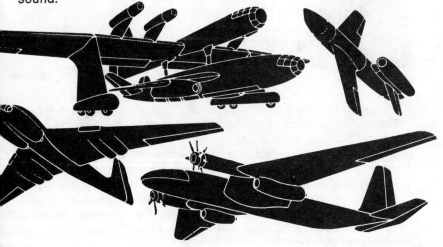

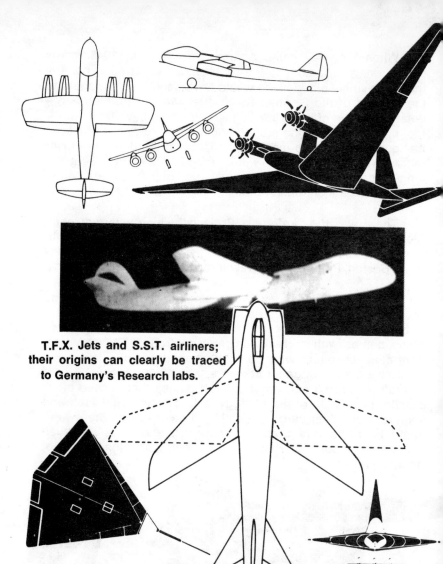

T.F.X. Jets and S.S.T. airliners; their origins can clearly be traced to Germany's Research labs.

Also there were passenger jets, a few of which are reproduced here. These plans had already progressed to the stage where models were being tested in the wind tunnels. It is interesting to see that the Americans adopted the German engine mountings on their later aircraft, but most startling of all is the Jumbo jet shown in these pages. Many of the Allied postwar developments originated right here in Germany's laboratories, as is evidenced by the following excerpts photographically reproduced from "America's Aircraft Year Book," an official publication. It speaks for itself.

As part of its comprehensive research program to exploit former enemy aeronautical developments, the Air Materiel Command's Technical Intelligence agency was using the services of some 86 top-flight German aviation scientists of World War II. Working side by side with American military and civilian aeronautical engineers in the laboratories of Wright Field, these German experts were being used, as were tons of captured enemy materiel, documents, blueprints and microfilm, to save American engineers the time they would devote to problems already investigated by the Germans. Their knowledge also helped the Americans to catch up and improve upon Germany's wartime advancement in such phases of aeronautical developments as rocket and jet power. Similar groups of former enemy technicians were employed in other parts of the country by various branches of the armed forces. At Fort Bliss, Texas, one group was working in connection with research on German V-2 rockets and other guided missiles. Others were working with the Army ordnance and engineer experts, and still others were working for the Navy in several fields of applied war research and development.

Among those in the German group at Wright Field were Rudolph Hermann, Alexander Lippisch, Heinz Schmitt, Helmut Heinrich, and Fritz Doblhoff and Ernst Kugel. Hermann was attached to the Peenemunde Research Station for Aerodynamics, where Germany's V-2 rockets were hatched and launched against England. A specialist in supersonics, he was in charge of the supersonic wind tunnel at Kochel in the Bavarian Alps. He also was a member of the group entrusted with Hitler's futuristic plans to establish a space-station rocket-refueling base revolving as a satellite about the earth at a distance of 4,000 miles—a scheme which he and certain high-ranking AAF officers in 1947 still believed to be feasible.

In order to break down the language difficulties in deciphering captured German documents, prominent educators were working with the AAF in compiling a new 75,000-word German-English dictionary intended to clarify German aeronautical terms and phrases. Supervising the project was Dr. Kurt L. Leidecker, on leave from the Behr-Manning Corporation and Rensselaer Polytechnic Institute, where he was assistant professor of modern languages and instructor of scientific German. Nearly half the contents of the new dictionary were to be new words. The Germans had nazified aeronautical terms formerly having classic roots, and had coined many new terms not found in any existing dictionary. Material for the dictionary was being extracted from broken enemy codes and from 250 tons of captured German air documents. Considerable value was attached to the widely heralded German ZWB (Central Organization for Scientific Reports) Index which contained important scientific documents. Included were many of the newer aeronautical terms and some applications of older words, which served as an aid to the project translators. Also helpful were German translations of American and British aeronautical terms found in captured documents, and the arbitrary words and phrases applied to German prototypes and equivalents of Allied equipment and accessories.

The German scientists worked voluntarily at Wright Field under special contracts as alien civilian employees of the War Department. Their salaries ranged from $2.20 to $11 a day, and were paid to their banks or families in Germany.

There are other developments never mentioned in any official book, namely the UFO and other even more devastating weapons. Why is no mention made of them officially? Is it because they were not found? Or that they were destroyed?

However, before proceeding with the UFO's there are a few more secret developments which must be covered and which, perhaps, you have never heard of before, — the death rays, the sun cannon, Pandora's Box and the Aeolus Bag.

ART BY FRANK BOLLE

The Sound Cannon

Once again, we find Hitler steering his scientists towards using nature, not opposing it. He had them harness two important elements, namely the power of the air and the power of the sun.

The first experiments started as early as 1943, on a lonely, rarely-visited mountain plateau in Tyrol. For a number of weeks scientists and specialists from the Reichsluftfahrtamt in Berlin (Office of Aeronautics) — of which Major Lusar, who reported about the German UFO programme, was also a member, had been busy setting up a camp, or more appropriately, a base. They were busy unpacking and assembling some odd-looking pieces of equipment. Huge crates arrived by truck from various parts of the Fatherland. Significantly again, many factories which were involved in this project were located underground in what is now Czechoslovakia. When all was assembled, there stood on that lonely, bleak plateau, high in the mist-shrouded mountains of Austria, a most fearsome weapon — the Sound Cannon. (see photograph reproduced here). It looks like a weird longish platform with an angular smoke stack that can be turned into horizontal positions and a fire place or boiler seems to be at the base of it. In actual fact it is a rigid steel combustion chamber in which methane and oxygen can be ignited under high pressure, with the ultimate aim of creating a series of powerful explosions at rapid intervals. The shock waves created by these explosions were to be directed, via the conical smoke stack against any aggressor, with a devastating force. The whole infernal principle was based on the knowledge that the shock waves of sound, generate a certain pressure upon objects which may be in their path. Thunderclaps with their earth-shaking after effects served as the father of thought, in this particular case.

Sonic booms as created by fast and high-flying jet aircraft can, in effect, damage buildings and burst ear drums. Sound, therefore, if strong enough, can kill. And so the reasoning went behind these tests. Why were they testing this device way up in the Alps? To the peasants below and around, it sounded like a thunderstorm and so created little suspicion.

The scientists had had hundreds of dogs and pigs trained to take the place of attacking Russian infantry. The animals were trained, Pavlovian style to run in a certain direction for their daily fodder, about 400 yards away. The day the experiment was started, they were once again headed for their troughs. The Sound Cannon had been erected behind some bushes. First came the dogs, then the pigs. There were no eaters at troughs that day; not one animal survived that 400 yard dash.

The dogs came first; at 150 yards distance the first salvo was fired, there was a terrific bang and then followed the shock waves. The dogs stood as if frozen to the ground. Suddenly they let loose a heart-rending howl and raced towards the troughs only to be hit by another round. The dogs had come within 50 feet of the sound cannon and not one of them survived that second shot. The pigs, still 100 yards away were paralyzed for hours. All suffered from disorientation effects, causing them to run helter skelter in each and every direction. None of them made it to the feeding troughs.

The sound cannon was used operationally against the Russians on the approaches to the Elbe River and against American aircraft close to Passau on the Danube — with the same results. (One wonders did Admiral Byrd suffer the same fate as the pigs when he gave orders to abort that Antarctic overflight after all his orientation instruments went haywire in 1947?). Illustration shows artist's conception of the Sound Cannon.

The Aeolus Bag

This New-Age weapon was used to fight off the seemingly endless hordes of Mongolians that were spewed forth from Asia's vast steppes. It used oxygen and hydrogen for combustion. The weapon's function was similar to an air compressor, commonly found on construction sites. If you have ever witnessed the concentrated power of pressurized air from a pneumatic tool or drill you will be able to appreciate the potential impact of the Aeolus Bag. It could stop a truck or a plane dead in its track before disintegrating it.

The Sun Cannon

Very early in the war, the Germans, well-versed in Greek mythology, built another contraption of note. This silent weapon consisted of a huge truck-mounted mirror able to be rotated at will. The sun's rays were to be collected, concentrated and sent back towards the sky, blinding enemy pilots and gunners, and so giving to the German fighters very easy pickings. Due to weather conditions over northern Europe, the weapon was seldom used "at home". However, a member of the Africa Corps reported it used on the ground on some occasions and with excellent results.

Pandora's Box

When first conceived Pandora's Box was thought of as an anti-aircraft weapon, but it proved to be most devastating on the ground. The SS used it against the Jewish uprising in the Ghetto of Warsaw.

The inventor was, in civilian occupation, a mining engineer. He simply re-created the dread of all coal miners — an underground coal dust explosion. The explosion literally razed any building from its foundations. (See illustration). None of these weapons were ever used by the allies in any of the 50 wars since the end of W.W. II. One could safely assume therefore that these weapons did not fall into allied hands, since every other German invention has been reproduced; from missiles to space flight and satellites, and each has been always loudly heralded as some scientific breakthrough by either Russia or Uncle Sam.

This brings to mind a glaring example of the "Brain Drain". Recently it was announced with great fanfare that a U.S. paint company had perfected a superb camouflage paint capable of absorbing radar waves or make them unintelligible. They must have either "re-invented" a German invention which had been long in U.S. hands, and probably at great expense to the U.S. taxpayer, or else they just pocketed the money for going through Hitler's files, for it was nothing more than the paint used on German planes at the end of the war.

There were also other fantastic developments in the purely conventional aircraft design. Reproduced here are a few of the planes on the drawing boards when Germany surrendered. The famous B.M.W. plant in Munich produced for Hitler the world's first supersonic jet bomber only 12 months after Hitler had requested it. It's range was to be 10,000 miles. Six jet engines were to give it the speed of sound at an altitude of over 50,000 feet. The plane's code name, the Horten XVIII, would have been rolling off the assembly lines in the summer of 1945. It was to have carried 8,000 pounds of explosives to

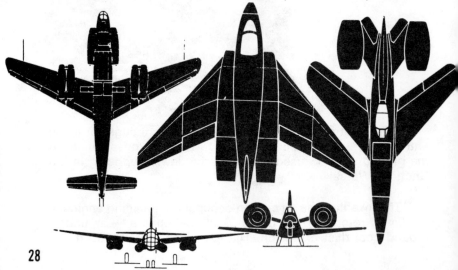

America and Russia and was designed to give the native population of these continents a taste of what it felt like to be at the receiving end of the "Liberators".

Hitler was an ardent believer in the teaching of Clausewitz and despite having under his control all of the above advanced technology and the atom bomb, he realised the necessity of having a certain amount of physical force to be able to occupy and control any given land-populated area. This Hitler lacked in April 1945 and hence his strategic withdrawal from Berlin.

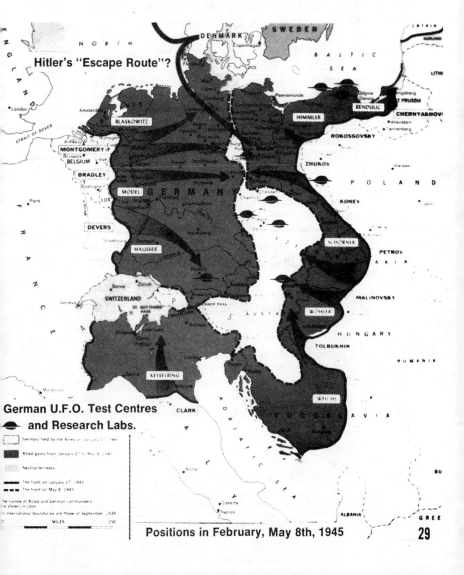

Hitler's "Escape Route"?

German U.F.O. Test Centres and Research Labs.

Positions in February, May 8th, 1945

With the advancing allied armies came teams of scientifically trained specialists, whose sole jobs were to hunt for German scientists and to ensure that their installations, laboratories and factories were not destroyed. The Americans were the cleverest and best organized in this field, capturing many "prize catches", and this, much to the chagrin and often anger, of the British, the French and especially the Russians. This great American "brain robbery" of the defeated enemy was so mind-boggling that a special dictionary for technical jargon of the aircraft industry alone had to be created by the captured Germans. It was comprised of over 75,000 separate terms and it made possible the exploitation of the stolen German patents. Wind tunnels, whole factories, all machines, every nut and bolt, including models, drawings and prototypes were shipped to America and to a lesser degree to the other allies. Top flight scientists were "invited" to work in the U.S. for $2.20 a day while being kept prisoners. In order to get cooperation, their starvation diets were kept "supplemented". Some were even offered citizenship as an inducement, or "war crimes" trials if they didn't produce. They included "Wernher von Braun"!

The Russians used methods only slightly different to those used by the Americans. On one particular occasion in an extremely well-coordinated plan conducted all over Soviet-occupied Germany, 275,000 specialists with their wives and children were hauled out of their beds in the early hours of the morning.

KIDNAPPING OF GERMAN SPECIALISTS

The raid was conducted in the Soviet Zone, 21st and 22nd October, 1946, all over central Germany by heavily armed troops, working to a minutely detailed plan. The specialists were forced to sign work agreements of five-year duration. Those who refused were taken in spite of their refusal. Women, children and even babies were taken. Protests were ignored or beaten down.

With few personal belongings, they were all shipped off to Russia. German factories were awaiting them, already dismantled and crated. There these specialists worked around the clock for three bowls of borscht soup and a slice of dark bread daily. In this way they were forced to help in bringing the Soviets, first, up-to-date and into the 20th Century, and then into the space age. With the further aid of U.S. Communist spies, Rosenberg, Greenglass et al the Russians were able to produce the first atom bomb. German science allowed them to produce Mig fighter-planes which were used to kill many Americans in Korea and later, in Vietnam.

The German scientists worked in about 40 different locations all over Russia:

40% in Kujbyschew — aircraft and jet engineer works
31% in Podberesje — aircraft design
6.5% in Moscow — radio, telephone technicians
4.5% in Tuschinow — pipelines
3% in Ostasckleow —
2% in Suchumi — Atomic research
1.5% in Leningrad — T.V. technicians

When the Germans protested as a group, they were shown documents, in English, signed by President Roosevelt of the United States, and by Winston Churchill, granting the Russians the express right to utilize any German person as they saw fit. Apparently these democratic leaders had no regard for human rights or liberties. These were the same men, who had wailed at Nuremberg, about the Germans utilizing forced labour in concentration camps. What hypocrites.

After their five year terms had been served, during which many had died and many were condemned to slave labour camps for life — camps such as "Workuta", the scientists were kept for another 2-3 years in quarantine, so that they would forget the projects they had worked on, no pencils, no paper was allowed them. What devils in human form. Sanctioned by the leaders of England and the U.S.A.

All submarine construction, torpedo development, tank-building and, of course, military rocket construction was performed by the forced, slave labour of the German top brains and thus was fulfilled the agreement made by the Allies, and in particular by the Americans, at conferences held in Potsdam and Yalta.

The Allies committed the greatest highjacking crime in all recorded history when they stole thirty railroad cars full of German patents. Stolen is the only word that fits this crime, for not a cent was ever paid to Germany in royalties or property rights. However, the true motives of both the East and West were soon revealed to the entire world. It was not humanitarian ideals that led to the "get Germany" war in 1939 but obviously it was outright theft and industrial-economic considerations. As soon as the Allies had in their hands the German specialists and had bombed their troublesome competitor (German industry) out of the world market place, (not a savoury method but an extremely effective one), (see photo copy of U.S. Steel Speech), they couldn't have cared less about freedom. There was no freedom of the press, freedom of speech or of opinion in Allied-occupied Europe and even today, thirty years later, there is still none.

U. S. Steel

President Here, Predicts Big Market In Europe For Postwar Rehabilitati

BY LARRY GUERIN

Europe will look to the United States for steel for rehabilitation for several years after the war because its own steel industries have been crippled by aerial warfare. Benjamin F. Fairless, Pittsburgh, president of the U. S. Steel Corporation, said in New Orleans today.

"Bombings have taken a heavy toll in Europe," he said. "If reports reaching us are accurate, then we are led to believe that the steel industry, if not destroyed, is seriously crippled. European countries will need steel for rebuilding. It is only logical to suspect that we will be called upon to produce steel for her needs.

"European requirements, together with substantially more business with South America than ever before, will keep the steel industry in this country humming for some time to come.

"The industry in this country is today producing all the steel it can possibly turn out. There is a need for even more but we do not have the man power or the facilities with which to produce it.

"U. S. Steel Corporation shipped 21,000,000 tons last year. This was a third of the nation's total output. The steel industry as a whole produced last year between 20,000,000 and 30,000,000 tons more ingots than it did during pre-war years.

"I don't like wars. But as a re-sult of the present war, the steel industry has shown tremendous advancements in the development of new products and new techniques. The ultimate development of these new ideas will take place after the war.

PLANTS FOR SOUTH

"I am enthusiastic about the future of the South, and I look for the establishment of new plants using fabricated steel for their products."

Mr. Fairless has been in the steel business for 32 years, and has been president of U. S. Steel since 1938. He is 55, and is here on an inspection tour of his firm's plant in New Orleans is the Bennett Manufacturing Co., on the

Jefferson Highway near Plauche.

He is accompanied by Mrs Fairless, George Wolfe, president of the U. S. Steel Export Co.; Robert Gregg, president of the Tennessee Coal, Iron and Railroad Co.; M. H. Geisking, vice-president of the same company, and E. D. LeMay, public relations director of the U. S. subsidiaries in the southeas sion.

Mr. Fairless was slated to i harbor facilities here toda will leave tomorrow for T

War and its aftermath always mean big profits for big business

It was also the victors who introduced at Nuremberg the "democratic" order that "Might was Right" and so hanged Europe's elite for alleged crimes, which similar crimes the victors were still committing daily, such as employing slave labour (P.O.W.'s), establishing and running concentration camps, (Dachau, Buchenwald, Auschwitz etc., but now with Allied guards), and expelling millions from their ancestral home lands, to name a few.

However, despite all the stealing, one prize catch eluded both the east and west. Germany's U.F.O. research scientists could not be found. At first, drunk with victory, this important factor was overlooked but as the hangover from booty hunting, rape and conquest came to an end, it was too late. That some key scientists were obviously missing became clear, and although some plants and their installations were located, the staff with their machinery and prototypes had disappeared. Even the test pilots had vanished.

The Allied Intelligence networks again became active, but now the singleness of purpose — to kill the Krauts — was missing. The Allies began to suspect and accuse each other of having captured the "last secret". They had agreed to divide the loot "honestly". Each Ally was to receive microfilm copies of each and every German patent and secret document, regardless of whom had captured them, and since each stated they had kept their side of the bargain, a deadlock was reached. This controversy, which took place in the utmost secrecy and on the highest level, suddenly took a new and alarming twist.

From Northern Europe, and especially from neutral Sweden, came reports of Flying Saucers, called by the Swedish Press, "German Secret Weapons". This caused a sensation not only in Europe but in the entire world.

Stories abounded about overflights by these strange objects at speeds and in formations which the Swedes had only seen during the latter days of the war. During intense German secret weapon development, many of these weapons were being tested in the then still safe Baltic area. This U.F.O. activity (as it soon became called), occurred at just about the same time as serious European, and especially North and South American newspapers and radio networks, were carrying sensational reports about Hitler.

It was being claimed that Adolf Hitler had never committed suicide but had escaped from the Bunker in Berlin via a "hospital tank", had been taken to Tempelhof airfield and there, with his wife, Eva Braun-Hitler, had transferred to one of Germany's fast jets and flown first to Denmark and then on to Norway. Both Denmark and Norway were still firmly in German hands. From Norway, Hitler and a mysterious group of people, making up an entire convoy, were claimed to have left for an unknown destination. Let us now investigate!

Whilst the last paragraph reads like a story out of a sensational publication, (the type usually dealing with crime and sex), nevertheless Time magazine issue of May 7th, 1945, (one day before the war was officially ended), gave space for the following article, and this seven days after Hitler's supposed suicide. Add to this the fact that the Press service from which this report emanated and was distributed, seems to be the same one or at least connected with, the Press service for which a certain Willy Frahm (now known as the retired Chancellor of West Germany, Willy Brandt) quite freely filed stories whilst in exile. Should this be the case then the report must be given added credence, for another of these exiles using this

Hitler Story

Along with the authentic news from the perishing Third Reich came a rash of rumors and "reports." The dizziest to reach print was whelped by the unreliable "Free German Press Service," operated in Stockholm by Germans who call themselves "*émigrés*." F.G.P.S.'s latest gasp:

The "Hitler" who was in Berlin was not Hitler at all. It was a Plauen grocer named August Wilhelm Bartholdy, whose face was his misfortune: he looked like the Führer. Grocer Bartholdy, said F.G.P.S., had been carefully coached and combed, then sent to Berlin "to die on the barricades. . . . He will act as Hitler's trump card, creating a hero legend around the Führer's death, while Hitler himself goes underground." To fasten the hoax on posterity, *Reichsbildberichterstatter* (Photographic Reporter for the Reich) Heinrich Hoffmann would "be on hand to film Hitler's last moment on the battlefield."†

70   TIME, MAY 7, 1945

† When Hoffmann was taking the real Hitler's picture in front of the Eiffel Tower in 1940, the Führer reportedly cracked: "Take this one, Hoffmann; then the next one in Buckingham Palace and the next in front of the skyscrapers."

service was Herbert Wehner, today a top West German politician. At this time he was known as one of Stalin's most active operators in the European underground and under constant surveillance by the Swedish Police as a "Soviet Agent".

These types of Press services were usually the mouthpieces of communist spy rings inside German-controlled Europe. They were organized and financed by the Soviet Komintern or K.G.B. Their sources of information were from secret communist cells operating vast guerilla and spy networks which the Russians had set up even before W.W. II. Usually their information was first hand.

The Reds were waiting for the day of Germany's defeat when they could then get away with "murder" by killing all anti-Communists and conveniently calling them Nazi-collaborators.

Local Man Sends Truman $5000 To Start a Capture-Hitler Fund

In the belief that Adolf Hitler is still alive and is being protected by his followers, Attorney William J. Brock today sent a certified check for $5000 to President Truman with the request it be used as the nucleus of a $500,000 fund for the capture of the former fuehrer. The attorney said the award would be made entirely at the President's discretion.

In his letter, Mr. Brock said:

"Newspaper comments from time to time seem to indicate the possibility that Adolf Hitler is still alive. His name is historically synonomous with evil. Hitlerism has soiled the pages of history, causing the death of millions of innocent persons, the destruction of property, and what is even worse, has caused a perversion of the sous of millions more. It would be tragic if the trail of blood, oppre-sion and foulness that he has left could again be followed by activation and further growth of Hitlerism upon his return from hiding.

"Since Hitler and his followers had been proven devoid of ideals and were, and still are, motivated by selfishness, greed and avarice, I feel his own followers would be tempted to turn Hitler over to Allied authorities provided the price is sufficiently large.

"I hereby tender the enclosed check for $5000 which I hope will form a nucleus for further sums to be contributed by public-spirited Americans for a fund to be offered as a reward to the person or persons causing the capture, apprehension and trial by the Allied Commission of Adolf Hitler. It would seem the sum of $500,000 would be a sufficient attraction for the most ardent adherent of Fuehrer Hitler."

Another very interesting article was one which appeared in many U.S. newspapers announcing the formation of a "Capture Hitler Fund"! This is only second to an incredible book written by one of America's senior diplomats, former Secretary of State Jimmy Byrnes, in which he reveals a lengthy conversation he had with Stalin about the touchy subject of Hitler's disappearance from the world scene, and confirms Stalin's belief that Adolf Hitler had not died in the Bunker in Berlin.

Reproduced here is a condensed version of an article which appeared in an American religious publication entitled "The Cross and The Flag" of date April 1948, and gives Stalin's response to a direct question from Mr. Byrnes about Hitler's whereabouts. It seems that even the highest echelons of the Allied governments were not convinced of Hitler's death, for any reports of Hitler having been seen were always thoroughly checked out.

Is Hitler Still Alive?

Former Secretary of State Jimmy Byrnes reveals in his new book entitled "Frankly Speaking" that it is the opinion of Joe Stalin that **Hitler is still alive.** The statement of Byrnes sounds more like a belated confession than an historical account. Says Byrnes in effect: "While in Potsdam at the Conference of the Big Four, Stalin left his chair, came over and clinked his liquor glass with mine in a very friendly manner. I said to him: **'Marshal Stalin, what is your theory about the death of Hitler?'** Stalin replied: **'He is not dead. He escaped either to Spain or Argentina.'**"

If anyone knows where Hitler is, outside of his intimate friends, it is Josef Stalin. It will be remembered that the American troops were ready to invade Berlin first, but at the order of Franklin D. Roosevelt, acting through Ike Eisenhower, the American troops were held back in order that Stalin might have the honor of capturing Berlin. What a deal! What a betrayal of the pride and dignity of the United States Army, and what an insult to the British Army which was also ready to move in with our troops.

There are numerous theories concerning what happened to Hitler. I list them below:

1. The publicized theory is that he was burned up during the bombing of Berlin.
2. He was captured by the Russians and is now a prisoner in Moscow.
3. He was captured by the Russians, tortured and then killed.
4. He was spirited away by certain Jewish extremists who desired to slaughter him as an act of revenge.
5. He was assassinated by one of his own aides who had accepted a large sum from Hitler's enemies and promised safety.
6. He committed suicide.
7. He commandeered a military plane and escaped with a staff of trusted compatriots.

Evidently Joe Stalin believes that the seventh theory is correct. I agree with Stalin in this theory. The most sensational neglect of a news story is in the fact that when Stalin told this to Byrnes it was not flashed across the world and given sensational display in the headlines of every daily newspaper on earth. It is still one of the most sensational pieces of news to come out. I will give you my reasons for believing that the first six theories are not well founded.

1. Just prior to the capture of Berlin, Hitler was in complete command of all military forces. Why did a man as brilliant and powerful as he was crawl down into a shelter and submit himself to cremation. This is il-

logical and unreasonable in the light of all that is known about Hitler.
2. Hitler was hated by the Russians more than any enemy that the Soviet had. He never would have submitted to being captured by them alive, and there was no reason why he should have been captured. Escape was really easy as far as he was concerned.
3. The argument which eliminates the second theory eliminates this one.
4. There were practically no Jews in Berlin when it was captured or prior to its capture. This theory seems far-fetched.
5. This theory might stand up were it not for the fact that only a few months prior to his disappearance certain corrupted friends had planted a bomb under his chair and somehow it did not go off at the proper moment, but went off after he left his chair, injuring him but not killing him. This made him very cautious and it is reasonable to believe that he was very alert at the time of his disappearance to betrayal within his own camp.
6. This theory is exploded by the fact that Hitler was a very courageous man. He never did anything to indicate physical or moral cowardice. It will be recalled that newsreels showed him walking freely and mixing freely with the crowds. A courageous man, whether he is wrong or right, whether he is a statesman or criminal, never commits suicide.
7. This theory stands up and there is any one of five or six places where he might be today. They include (a) *Argentina;* (b) *Spain;* (c) *Ireland;* (d) *Sweden;* (e) *Africa;* (f) *Portugal;* (g) *Switzerland.*

Hitler was known to have many, many followers in all of these countries. It will be remembered when Stalin was about to overrun and undermine Spain, and his followers were burning the churches, that Hitler sent an abundance of help to Franco, and Franco evidently felt under lasting obligation to Hitler.

Whatever the truth may be concerning this matter, it is not to be overlooked that Hitler, Mussolini and Roosevelt left the stage of action within a few weeks of each other. Mystery still surrounds the passing of Roosevelt. Thus, these 'three rulers,' who were perhaps three of the most powerful men that ever lived, disappeared from public life shrouded with mystery. It is now a matter of common knowledge that Mussolini was hanged by a Communist mob. The same people who hung Mussolini and spat upon him and rolled his body in the gutter in such a barbaric manner that the church authorities protested — it is now a matter of common knowledge that the same people and leaders who lynched Mussolini without a trial are now the leaders of the movement to make Italy Communist and turn it over to Tito and Stalin.

To those who believe that Hitler is dead I submit the following questions:

1. Who saw him die?
2. Why hasn't someone been able to produce a piece of metal or a bone or a tooth filling that remained after his alleged cremation?
3. Why did he voluntarily wait to be consumed when he had so many opportunities for escape?
4. Why does his personal aviator admit that he flew him out of Germany and turned him over to another plane?
5. Of course, the $54 question is: Why did Stalin tell Mr. Byrnes that he was convinced that Hitler was still alive? Although Stalin is perhaps the world's biggest liar, there would be no object in his not telling the truth concerning this matter. Stalin guessed Spain or Argentina. My guess is Argentina. The Argentine people were very friendly to Germany. The Argentine has a large German population, many of whom were pro-Hitler. Peron has made it safe for Mussolini's son and now his family.

THE SATIRE OF FATE

The satire of the passing of time in the hands of fate lies in the fact that we are now in Hitler's boots in one respect. We are trying to figure out how to push back Stalin.

When the Jew lynch mob which runs the Nuremberg Court caused the top generals of Germany to be virtually lynched without an appeal to a higher court and in violation to America's sense of justice, one of the generals said, as he was about to be hanged "Some day Stalin will do this to you."

It is interesting to note that the presiding judge at Nuremberg, a high class Supreme Court Justice from Iowa, recently announced that if he had known the facts he never would have gone to Germany. He criticized and virtually condemned the whole set-up. (See editorial elsewhere in this magazine entitled "Judge Gets a Stomachful".)

We may need a knowledge of Hitler's experience some day if we are to prevent Russia from overrunning the world. We need to know why Hitler failed to stop Stalin in order that we may profit by his mistakes.

As the truth comes out we begin to discover reports being made by the most conservative journalists that the war could have been avoided and that by a statesmanlike manipulation Hitler and Stalin could have weakened themselves on each other without destroying all of Europe and without involving us in a debt which now threatens inflation and depression. Strange enough, England and France, our two chief allies, are suffering almost as much as Germany, although they were, along with us, alleged victors.

If Hitler is still alive I hope it will some day be discovered and he will be permitted to tell his experience. Some experience! It could be that both Franco and Peron are profiting by his mistakes. They have established governments strong enough to eliminate Communism, free enough to give opportunity to the people, and sincere enough to protect the churches. Let us hope and pray that a strong central government will never be necessary in the U.S.A., but if we have to choose, may it be God's last will that as between a strength dedicated to Stalin and a strength dedicated to Jesus Christ, it may be the latter.

Oberst Skorzeny was a famous German Commando leader and a personal friend of Hitler. Hitler entrusted him with many daring missions, such as the rescuing of Mussolini from his mountain-top prison, and the arresting of Vice-Regent Horthy of Hungary from the Castle in Budapest, at a time when the Castle was surrounded by thousands of Hungarian elite troops. Skorzeny was repeatedly interrogated by the American C.I.C. and even as late as 1947-48, about his alleged role in the escape of Hitler!

Did Hitler and some of his closest men indeed survive the Third Reich? This question is of world significance, and it is with this in mind that the following articles are quoted, and some are reproduced in photo copy form for those readers who are multilingual.

Of all the articles and the versions of Hitler's escape from his embattled bunker in Berlin, the following seems the most plausible: In the German-language book "Das Ende des Hitler Mythos", page 339, reference is made to a series of events which completely negate the claims of the suicides of

LA SUPUESTA FUGA DE HITLER

VARSOVIA ? — (A. P.) —
El . . . Argentino "Wiecrel"
. . . un artículo citando al ex
. . . común de los SS, capi-
. . . Peter Baumgart, como diciendo que Hitler y Eva Braun
. . . a Estados Unidos a bor-
do de un submarino, dos días
. . . de la caída de Berlín, en
1945.

Baumgart fué citado en forma
similar por el mismo diario, en
octubre del año pasado, diciendo

. . . lo mismo; pero, en esa opor-

Tanquista alemán dice haber visto escapar a Hitler

MUNICH, 17 (UP). — Un
tanquista alemán de 24 años de
edad, que no quiso revelar su
nombre por temor a represa-
lias nazis, declaró bajo juramen-
to que vió a Hitler escapar de
la Cancillería en un tanque-
ambulancia el 29 de Abril de
1945, es decir, el día que el
Fuehrer se suicidó.

Esta historia ha provocado
poco interés oficial.

PRETENDE HABER VISTO HITLER QUE HUIA

NUREMBERG, Alemania, 6
(AP).— Funcionarios del Servi-
cio de Inteligencia del Ejército
de Estados Unidos encontraron
a otro alemán que pretende ha-
ber visto a Hitler y Eva Braun
escapar de Alemania. Arthur
Frederick Angelotte Mackensen,
ex piloto de la fuerza aérea alemana, afirmó a los oficiales que
él vió a Hitler y a Eva escapar
por avión de Berlín hacia Dinamarca, a fines de abril de
1945.

Mackensen fué arrestado en
Molfratshausen, cerca de Munich, por una información pro-
porcionada por una muchacha
alemana.

Los oficiales dijeron que re-
latos similares les han sido he-
chos en el pasado, pero nunca

ZIGZAG
16 Enero 48

¿HITLER EN DINAMARCA?

Durante el proceso que se realizó
en la ciudad de Varsovia, el capitán
Peter Baumgart declaró que había
llevado en un avión a Hitler y a un
grupo de amigos de éste a Dinamarca el día 28 de abril de 1945, . . .
pes de los Aliados. Añade que le-
vante vuelo en el . . .
damm y aterrizó a 70 . . . metros
del río Elter, en Dinamarca. Según
su declaración el Fuehrer le entre-
gó al aterrizar un cheque por 20,000
marcos. Baumgart aparece en esta
fotografía con uniforme de aviador,
tal como se presentó en el juicio que
se le sigue en Varsovia en su con-
dición de miembro de la organiza-
ción hitlerista de las S. S. —inicia-
les con que se designaba a la
"Schutz-Staffel", la fuerza organi-
zada y férreamente disciplinada por
Heinrich Himmler para la protec-
ción del Fue . . .

Spanish newspaper reports about Hitler's escape

Hitler and Eva Braun. These suicides are usually stated to have happened at the Fuhrer Bunker, Berlin, April 30th, 1945, 3.30 p.m. In the above book it is claimed that Hitler was seen at 4.15 p.m. on that same day. Eyewitnesses gave their accounts under oath. Hitler either made a Christ-like resurrection, three quarters of an hour after his "death" or he had left the Bunker alive and with a plan.

According to further evidence contained in press reports emanating from Munich and appearing in the pages of "Diario Ilustrado" of Santiago, Chile issue of 18th January, 1948, "on 30th of April, 1945, Berlin was in dissolution but little of that dissolution was evident at Tempelhof airfield. Ground support organizations, such as radio, radar as well as harbour and riverboat direction were functioning at peak efficiency. Take-offs and landings were handled smoothly. The airspace was crowded. Every six minutes a plane landed and ten planes took off every hour, and all of this with a city under siege. Highspeed German fighters and jets could be seen circling about to secure airspace and consequently Tempelhof runways had received only minor damage. The sound of machine-gun fire could be heard in the distance. Radio operators had received reports that the Russians had advanced to the Koch and Oranian Strasse. Contact to the city's centre had been interrupted. Two alternatives remained, escape by air from Tempelhof or capture by the advancing Soviet troops".

"At 4.15 p.m. a JU52 landed, and S.S. troops directly from Rechlin for the defence of Berlin disembarked, all of them young, not older than 18 years. The gunner in the particular plane was an engineer by the name of B....... whom I had known for a number of years and for whom I had endeavoured to get exemption from military service. He sought to tank up and leave Berlin as quickly as possible. During this re-fuelling interval Mr. B....... was suddenly elbowed in the ribs by his radio operator with a nod to look in a certain direction. At about 100-120 metres he saw a sleek Messerschmitt Jet Model 332. (The reporters must have made a mistake here, it could only have been an ARADO 234 — a mistake not difficult to understand since secrecy was the hallmark of the Nazi Regime. This Turbojet had a range of 4,000 km.) Mr. B....... and the radio operator saw and without any doubt whatsoever, standing in front of the jet, their Commander in Chief, Adolf Hitler, dressed in field-grey uniform and gesticulating animatedly with

Arado Ar 234

some Partyfunctionaries, who were obviously seeing him off. For about ten minutes whilst their plane was being refuelled the two men observed this scene and around 4.30 p.m. they took to the air again. They were extremely astonished to hear during the midnight military news bulletin, some seven and a half hours later that Hitler had committed suicide".

It was during this military news broadcast that Admiral Donitz announced that he was taking over as the new Commander-in-Chief. This same bulletin was broadcast over the German civilian radio network and Dr. Goebbels reported that the Fuhrer had entered Valhalla, (that mystical place in ancient Nordic sagas where heroes dwell after death).

Upon questioning, the engineer Mr. B........ denied the possibility of error on his part and reiterated that on April 30th, 1945 at 4.15 p.m., whilst refuelling his plane at Tempelhof airport, and in the bright light of the setting sun he saw Adolf Hitler, and at a time when it was no longer possible to reach the Reichskanzlei (Hitler's Bunker). When Mr. B........ first heard the news reports he concluded that Hitler had died in an airplane crash." This particular report by Mr. B........ with all the sensational content, was never published in the English-speaking press.

The Soviet Information Office reported on May 3rd, 1945, that Hitler's servant, Fritsche had been captured and interrogated by the Soviets and had stated that Hitler, Goebbels and the new Chief of the General Staff, General of the Infantry, Krebs, had committed suicide. Lt. Heimlich of the American

C.I.C., whose responsibility it was to check all rumours and reports, all sightings and evidence regarding the whereabouts or the death of Hitler, reached the conclusion that Hitler, Eva Braun and Martin Bormann were still alive and that there existed not one iota of proof that Hitler had actually died.

The report (INS) further stated that according to investigations by the American authorities it would have been relatively simple to escape from Berlin, whilst experts pointed to the almost impossible task of burning a corpse in the open air by just dousing it with a can of gasoline and not leave behind some recognisable evidence.

It is a fact that a working party made up of American, British, French and Russian soldiers did find a ditch which produced two hats, supposedly belonging to Hitler, and also a pair of panties bearing Eva Braun's initials, but no corpses or parts of corpses.

This is where Hitler's hats and Eva Braun's panties were found. (Allied investigators)

41

Much has been written regarding identification through medical and dental records and Hitler has been much in the news in this respect. A recent report by the Canadian Broadcasting Corporation makes interesting reading. On the programme "As it Happens" on September 17th, 1974 at 7:15 p.m., a Prof. Dr. Ryder Saguenay, oral surgeon from the Dental Faculty of the University of California at Los Angeles revealed the facts that Hitler had ordered a special plane to leave from Berlin with all medical and dental records, and especially X-rays, of the top Nazis and for an unknown destination, and that any drawings, charts and other evidence which have been presented, regarding Hitler's dental status; have been drawn from MEMORY by the dental assistant to Hitler's dentist, the latter who was himself never found.

To fully appreciate the importance of the above evidence, the situation of Germany at the end of the war must be taken into account. Planes were scarce, but apparently not too scarce for Hitler to decide it was of great importance to use one to fly medical and dental records to some unknown place. If Hitler had been contemplating suicide why would he have bothered to remove such vital evidence? To where were they flown and why did he feel it was necessary to remove all traces of such identifying material? Unless the "suicide" was a well-thought out ruse to confuse the Allies whilst Hitler was escaping.

Tanquista alemán dice haber visto escapar a Hitle

There are a few other reports from the Spanish-speaking press which deserve mention and reproduced here is one as it appeared in Editorial "Zig Zag". Santiago, Chile, on 16th January, 1948. It seems that on April 30th, 1945, a Peter Baumgart (FlugKapitan — Flight Captain), took Adolf Hitler, his wife Eva Braun, as well as a few loyal friends by plane from Tempelhof airport to Tondern in Denmark (still firmly in German hands). From Tondern, where Baumgart landed, the Fuhrer's party continued in a new plane with another crew, to Kristiansund in Norway, also still in German hands. There a German submarine convoy was waiting to receive its unusual "cargo". In the meantime the Junkers which had brought the Fuhrer returned to Tondern, circled the airfield and dropped a message to the effect that the Fuhrer had reached his destination safely. This unusual method of communicating was chosen, so as to keep radio silence and not attract undue notice. (From Mattern, U.F.O. Letzte Geheimwaffe des III Reiches page 50-51).

42

Another dimension is added to this story when comparing some of the statements made by Erich Kempka who had been in Hitler's employ, as chief of his carpool since 1932. In his book "Ich habe Adolf Hitler verbrannt" — "I burnt Hitler", page 109, he recounts that after some confused telephoned conversations with Gunsche (Hitler's personal adjutant), Gunsche shouted at him, wide-eyed and rather theatrically — "The Chief is dead". Kempka stated how shocked he felt and then how he asked Gunsche how could it have happened since he had spoken to Hitler just the day before when he, Hitler, was completely well and completely controlled. In the same book on page 139 there is further information which all points to a well-conceived plan. A German submarine commander had stated under interrogation by the American C.I.C. that he was under orders since 25th April, 1945, to be at constant readiness, "Besonderen Verfugung", under immediate control of the Fuhrer. At Bremen this submarine commander declared that at least 10 other submarine commanders had received the same order!

Further, the C.I.C. found that twelve Flight Captains had been issued a valid secret order from the Fuhrerhauptquartier (Hitler's H-Q.) to be in a constant state of readiness for Hitler's departure.

Gross Admiral Donitz has always figured in developments surrounding Hitler's whereabouts, and Donitz was Hitler's successor. The American writer, Malcolm X refers to him in his book "We Want You? Is Hitler Alive?", page 10, and claims that Donitz knew about Hitler's plans and was instrumental in his escape to an oasis in South America.

Mattern, in his German version of the U.F.O. Story, repeatedly quotes Donitz as playing a key role in the Fuhrer's plans. On page 15 he reports excerpts from one of Donitz's speeches at a graduation ceremony to naval cadets in Kiel, in 1944: "The German navy has still a great role to play in the future. The German navy knows all hiding places for the navy to take the Fuhrer to, should the need arise. There he can prepare his last measures in ("aller Ruhe") complete quiet".

Michael Bar-Zohar speaks of the role of Donitz — "The Avengers" page 99. Essentially, Bar-Zohar corroborates Michael X and Mattern. Excerpts below.

Michael Bar-Zohar speaks of the role of Donitz

In 1943 Admiral Doenitz had declared: "The German U-boat fleet is proud to have made an earthly paradise, an inpregnable fortress for the Fuehrer, somewhere in the world."

He did not say in what part of the world it existed, but fairly obviously it was in South America.

As far back as 1933, when the Nazi Party had come to power, the new masters of the Reich had made a special effort to spread their doctrine in South American countries. For several reasons, these countries presented a fertile field. There were large German colonies strongly established in many parts of Latin America. Several hundred thousand Germans or people of German stock were settled in Brazil. At Blumenau and Florianópolis, in the federal state of Santa Catarina, everything was, and still is, reminiscent of Germany—the countryside, the style of the houses, the appearance of the people, their speech. It was the same in several regions of Argentina. In the capital, Buenos Aires, in Tucumán, Formosa, Córdoba, and Cordier, in the Gran Chaco and the vastness of the *Paraná Misiones,* and at San Carlos de Bariloche, a bit of Switzerland in the southern hemisphere, with its pine trees and snow-clad mountainside—at all these places German colonies had settled and expanded with amazing rapidity. In Paraguay, tens of thousands of German immigrants had cleared and cultivated virgin areas to the east of the Asunción and had given their new towns names like Hohenau to remind them of their origins. Another wave of German immigrants had spread over the southern part of Chile, the region round the towns of Osorno and Valdivia, and the island of Chiloé, as well as settling in the capital, Santiago. Many more had gone to Peru, Uruguay, and other Latin American countries.

Having made an initial study of the mind of Hitler and having some understanding of his modus operandi we can now move into another area of this story. What are the other indications, which point to where, why, when and how? Let us examine some of the statements made during Hitler's career.

Hitler never tied the success of his mission on the sole fate of Germany. He fully realised, and early in his career, that Germany proper could be over-run by his enemies. He said right at the beginning of the war and during the conquest of Poland, "And if our enemies should inundate (uberschwemmt) all of Germany, we shall then fight on from abroad, we will never capitulate." And another statement from no less

44

a book than "Mein Kampf", German version, 1938, page 470: "The battle that rages today is for very high goals. A culture fights for its existence, that encompasses the heritage of ancient Greece and modern Germandom as well . . ."

Again, we see that Hitler saw the struggle as a global one even before the war. He had written Mein Kampf in 1923-24. On page 475, of the same volume he states further: "Certainly the world is approaching a great upheaval. It can only be around one single issue; will it be favourable to the Aryan people or will it benefit only the eternal Jew?"

In these sentences can be found a very clear indication that Hitler felt, as far back as 1923-24 that the struggle, his struggle, (which, incidentally, is the literal translation of the words "Mein Kampf") was not for Germany alone but for all Aryan man, or to put it in simple language, for the existence of the white man.

It is evident from Hitler's alliance with "yellow" Japan and his collaboration and active support with many non-white independence movements, such as the Arabs, the Caucassus tribes, the Cossacks and also India, that he was never the narrow-minded, racist bigot allied propagandists have tried to brain-wash the world into believing. The German general, Beck, once said about Hitler, "This man has no fatherland". It is important we approach this entire question with an absolutely open mind, for only then will we be able to unravel this Hitler-U.F.O. connection.

Had Hitler been a narrow-minded, nationalist politician, a mustachioed dictator who experienced his thrills by ranting and raving at large crowds of cowed followers driven to mass rallies at bayonet point, then his end would seem explainable. He was far more than that, namely a prophet, with global vision much in the cast of the prophets of old who have been recorded and revered in the old Testament by both Christians and Jews. He was born into German-speaking central Europe, that's all. An accident of fate. Undoubtedly, he would have preached the same eloquent sermon had he been born in France or England.

On July 20th, 1944 Skorzeny arrived at Hitler's Headquarters bringing with him the liberated Mussolini. This visit coincided with the one and only nearly-successful attempt on Hitler's life. Hitler made to Skorzeny a most significant statement. "I begin to doubt whether the German people are worthy of my ideals". This statement again reveals Hitler's detachment from Germany and points up the mentality of a universal-thinking individual. It must be granted, that indications are present that Hitler was ready to continue the struggle from outside Germany. But how, and with what methods and weapons? Before we continue we must take another look at the suicide plot.

1. The bodies of Hitler and Eva Braun were never produced.

2. The items introduced as "evidence" are only circumstantial; two of Hitler's hats, 1 pair of panties with the initials E. B. and a few bones. (There were millions of bones lying all over Germany as the result of the mass-killing by the Allied aerial bombing)

3. The bloodstains found on the furniture in Hitler's quarters in the Bunker were not of his blood type.

4. Hitler was not suicide prone. On the contrary, only a few days earlier after he had heard of the suicide of the Mayor of Leipzig and his family, he had condemned suicide as cowardly and unbecoming to a National Socialist.

5. The most important witnesses and the men closest to Hitler have never been found, e.g. Bormann, Stumpfegger, Gunsche et al.

6. Hitler, by his very nature, and his unfailing belief in his mission, (one of global and not national dimensions), would tend to continue the struggle from elsewhere.

7. There are too many reports and sightings, eye witness reports and even evidence that the suicide attempt was a brilliantly-successful, carefully-staged scenario. A typical Hitler production.

In view of the above summation, we can assume that there was indeed a contingency plan.

One of the iron-clad rules of wartime Nazi Germany was to never let anyone, however high their position or rank, know more about a plan or operation than was absolutely necessary to the execution of his or her particular contribution to the overall whole. This rule applied to all and even to men like Himmler who was Chief of the S.S. and who by the end of the war, commanded vast military forces on the eastern front. Himmler had known Hitler since his earliest days and even he could not comprehend the absolute calm and certainty of final victory that Hitler displayed in those terrible last days in the Bunker in Berlin. He saw, when he tabled his ever more devastating reports about lost ground, enemy advances, bombing damage etc. how Hitler would listen attentively and quietly. This led him to speculate aloud and come to the conclusion "The Fuhrer has some kind of a plan" — reported in Trevor Roper's book "Hitler's Letzte Tage" on page 101.

There are other indications that even very high level military types, such as General Keitel and Jodl were not privy to all secrets. An April 22nd, 1945, these two men received orders to leave for the Obersalzberg (Hitler's famous "Alpine Redoubt" about which we will speak later). Although loyal to the very end to their Commander-in-Chief, they did not want to die in the "Rat Trap" as they called the Bunker in Berlin. Consequently, they tried to persuade Hitler to leave with them. A heated debate ensued, according to the ever-present stenographer, Hergesell, and even a forceful abduction of Hitler to the Alpine fortress was considered by the two top generals. Finally Bormann, one of the few who apparently was in the know about the plan, persuaded them otherwise, and they left without Hitler.

Dr. Josef Goebbels, one of the most brilliant followers and exponents of Hitler, seems also to have been initiated to some degree, in the final phase. He had a three hour meeting with Hitler in those hectic last days and left the meeting calling out "Mein Fuhrer was sind Sie gross" — "My Fuhrer, what a great man you are". A few days later in a radio broadcast he made a number of interesting statements and one in particular which referred to new Secret Weapons, so fantastic "they made my heart beat more quickly when I saw them".

There are also some statements he made to his secretary on April 22nd, 1945, as reported in the book "Mit Goebbels bis zum Ende", Durer Verlag, Buenos Aires ". . . We want to see if under these circumstances the Americans will shoot us in the back". A few days later Goebbels gave a further highly-significant glimpse of what was planned when he said "May God protect our Fuhrer during the approaching danger" — reported also in the above-mentioned book. Was Goebbels referring to the underwater journey to the paradisical oasis in South America? How much clearer could we be told of what was afoot?

Maybe in Hitler's own words? On February 24th, 1945 Hitler made a prophetic speech at the end of which he said these words:— "In this war there will be no victors and no vanquished either, but only the dead and the survivors. The last battalion however, will be a German one". A further definition can be obtained by Hitler's remark, towards the end of the war, that ". . . the inevitable and automatic clash between east and west will come sooner or later and we (the Germans) will then be and act as the proverbial tip of the scale".

Should there still be some doubt in the reader's mind as to whether there was, in fact, "something cooking" in Adolf Hitler's fertile brain in those days when his world around him was going up in dust, flames and smoke, then read this. Germany's legendary female flyer, Hanna Reitsch, holder of many world records, first rocket plane jet pilot, daredevil of the air and one of the Fuhrer's favourite people, had voluntarily accompanied one of Germany's top men — Ritter von Greim, to embattled Berlin. They flew over the Soviet lines in order to get into the beleaguered capital and were hit by Russian anti-aircraft fire. Ritter von Greim was hit by shrapnel and badly wounded. Hanna Reitsch managed to wrestle the controls of the floundering aircraft out of the hands of von Greim and landed the aircraft in Berlin's famous Unter den Linden Boulevard.

In the previously-quoted book of Trevor Roper, "Hitler's Letzte Tage", page 146, mention is made of a telephone conversation which took place on April 28th, 1945 at Hitler's headquarters, between Ritter von Greim and his subordinate, General Koller, who was in Furstenberg. "It goes something like this" said General Koller "He, (von Greim) would be lost. Gen-

Koller offered his condolences about Greim's condition, his wounds, and his seemingly useless promotion to new Chief of the German Luftwaffe (after Goring's firing). He bemoaned the state of things generally and the future of Germany, in particular. He also reiterated his doubts about being able to do anything with the Luftwaffe. Then he paused. He expected a similarly gloomy echo from the Fieldmarshall on the other end of the line. But the world was still full of surprises for Gen. Koller. Life in the Bunker Headquarters seemed even more surreal than his experiences at Furstenberg. Koller was astounded when instead of lamentation of impending defeat, he heard an optimistic analysis of the future, and even promise of an inevitable German victory. "Just wait", said the new Chief of the hard-pressed Luftwaffe. "Don't despair. **All will be well! The presence and optimism of the Fuhrer have given me new hope. The Bunker affects me like a fountain of youth**". Koller listened in disbelief and was incredulous. He just could not understand it at all.

So the optimism in Germany in these last days was spoken from the mouth of Goebbels, a brilliant doctor of jurisprudence, the Reichsminister and the hero of Berlin. The man who had wrestled the communist-controlled workers of Berlin out of the clutches of the false prophet's of Moscow and delivered them to the Fuhrer as a gift to Germany's inner healing. A level-head and a first-rate brain. Also from Heinrich Himmler, the cold realist, a top cop of Germany, holding the same position and wielding even greater power, than the late J. Edgar Hoover had held in the United States. And lastly, from Fieldmarshall Ritter von Greim's conversation with a General Staff Officer. All these men had had lifelong careers and training in the martial arts and were cool, non-emotional Prussians to the core. From the above, there can be only one conclusion and that is that Hitler did not commit suicide. Hitler did not die.

That there was a drama could hardly be denied, as evidenced by the article (reproduced earlier) from Time magazine, but weighing all the evidence, an escape from Berlin is certainly more likely than a suicide.

We have now covered almost every loose end and woven the loose strands into a more or less logical pattern. Now there remains only the how and where? Hitler escapes! Why?

Why were the secret weapons not used in the battle for Germany's survival? Many of them were, but there was a standard requirement in German military thinking that demanded that for every new weapon introduced, a defence had to be introduced with it. A sensible safety measure in case any weapon ever fell into enemy hands which could then quickly be copied and used against Germany. Thus, when radar was introduced, radar jamming devices were introduced at the same time. When fast jet planes were brought in, (200 kilometers faster than the fastest Allied planes in existence or in the planning stage), ground to air defence missiles were concurrently introduced.

It might interest the reader to have a look at this array of advanced technology, unparalleled in variety and ingenuity even to this day. The photographs shown here are of operational types only. Some of the "planned" hardware is also shown in order to give the reader a quick look at how far ahead National Socialist Germany was in 1945 compared with the rest of the world.

German U.F.O. being serviced. Conventional propulsion system.

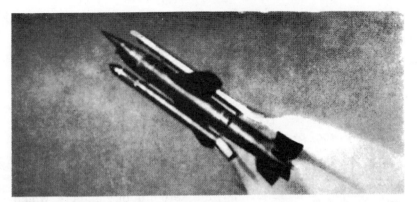

Anti-aircraft, ground to air rockets would have completely stopped Allied air activities over Germany after June, 1945

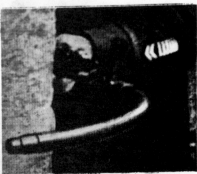

Flying People. Jet-powered back-packs — called "Himmelsturmer" — Sky stormer. Designed for mountain troops and for leaping across rivers

Intercontinental missiles were already a fact and although stolen by both the U.S. and Russia after the surrender in 1945 it took them another 15 years to come up to the German level, even though they were using many of the "captured" scientists. This brings us back to the actual story of the U.F.O. mystery.

Germany had U.F.O.'s as early as 1940. We find photographic proof of the existence of flying prototype models. Reproduced here are two photographs of two different U.F.O. designs, both operating on the electromagnetic propulsion method of Victor Schauberger, (also the inventor of the implosion motor), and produced by the Kertl firm of Vienna IV, which was then part of the greater German Reich.

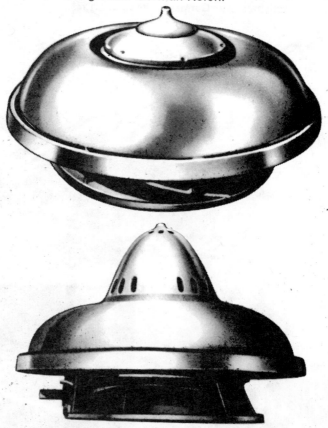

These are the famous smokeless, soundless, Schauberger Models. Note similarity to real U.F.O. shown in A.C. Roberts Photo

Below are reproduced a series of actual photographs of a U.F.O. photographed in flight over New Jersey in 1958 by George J. Stock of Passiac, N.J., courtesy August C. Roberts Wayne, N.J. The similarity to one of the Schauberger models is self-evident and is conclusive enough proof to most people of the German origin of the U.F.O.'s. However there is more.

This photo courtesy August C. Roberts

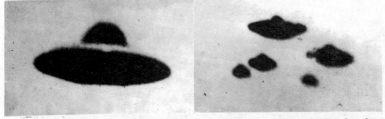

Photographed by A. Birch, February, 1964. Mosborough, England.

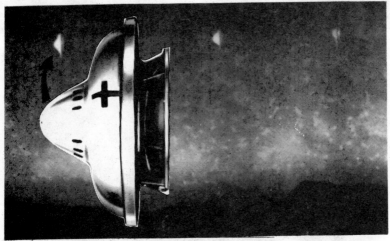

U.F.O. over Austria 1950

Photographed by Bruno Ghibandi, 27th April, 1961, Pescara, Italy. 53

U.F.O.'s were seen by American and German night fighters and bomber pilots over Germany in 1943-45. The Americans called them Kraut meteors and were scared of them. Even the top brass knew about their existence, as is indicated in the book entitled "Der Weltraum Ruckt Uns Naher", Blanvalet Verlag, by Major Keyhoe the famous U.F.O. investigator, Chapter III. Major Keyhoe says the U.S. infiltrated 600 scientists into Bohemia, in tank crew uniforms, in 1945, to check over some of the U.F.O. bases.

German Flying Saucer — called Kraut Meteor — during night flights in 1943-44.

Focke-Wulf 190 fighter plane in foreground. U.F.O. shooting straight upwards at tremendous speed. Over Austrian Alps 1944. Rare photograph.

Following is a letter from a lady, still alive and personally known to the authors which we have translated into free English. The lady attests to having been one of the first and top secretaries in the S.S. Reichssicherheitshauptamt working in the anteroom of one of the most powerful men in Nazi Germany — S.S. Amtschef III Ohlendorf (the subject of many books and articles since the end of the war). The lady letter writer states that one day in 1938 a young scientist came into her office clutching a document, neatly typed and comprised of about 60 pages. The young man said that the contents were a revolutionary new approach to the aircraft propulsion problem.

mir sagte, hat er den Mr. X während seiner USA-Reise persönlich kennengelernt und ■. meint, daß X Holländer sei. Die darin aufgeführte Meinung, daß die UFO's auf das Schauberger'sche Prinzip zurückgehen, teile ich nicht, weil Herr Schauberger auf einer anderen Grundlage aufbaute und ja auch nicht mitgenommen wurde. Die UFO's arbeiten auf elektromagnetischer Basis. Ab September 193■ war ich im RSHA (damals noch SD-Hauptamt) als eine der ersten ■■■■■■ tätig und habe das Vorzimmer des Amtschef III, Ohlendorf, betreut. 1939 so um die Zeit des Kriegsbeginns erschien eines Tages bei uns ein freundlicher etwa 3o-jähriger junger Mann bei uns und gab eine etwa 5o-6o-seitige Niederschrift ab, die ich seitens des SD Unterstützung bei der Durchführung gegeben werde, die er aber nicht bekam, weil unsere "Akademiker" das nicht begriffen und als "verrückt" abtaten, worüber ich damals empört war, obwohl ich es nicht verstanden habe. Neben dem Chef und seinem Vertreter habe auch ich die Niederschrift gelesen - mit atemloser Spannung. Darin war genau beschrieben, wie man machen könnte, wenn "Luftelektrizität und Erdmagnetismus" in der beschriebenen Form verwendet würden. Begriffen hatte ich es damals nicht, aber der Inhalt blieb in meinem Gehirn wie ein Steckschuß sitzen. Diese Schrift lag einige Wochen bei mir im Panzerschrank, bis eines Tages der Herr freudestrahlend erschien und sagte"Frau ■.kann ich meine Niederschrift wieder haben, ich habe jemand gefunden, der sich der Sache annehmen will."
Als 1954 im Blanvalet-Verlag das von Major Keyhoe aus Veranlassung des Pentagon geschriebene Buch unter dem Titel "Der Weltraum rückt uns näher" erschien konnte ich in Kapitel VIII lesen, daß der "kanadische Untertassenforscher Wilbert Smith festgestellt habe, daß diese Dinger auf magnetischer Basis arbeiten würden, mußte ich sofort wieder an diese Niederschrift von 1939 denken. In Kapitel III schreibt Keyhoe, daß "diese Dinger 1944 der Schrecken der amerikanischen Nachtjäger gewesen seien und von diesen Sauerkraut-Meteore genannt wurden. 1945 wurden 600 amerikanischen Wissenschaftler in Panzeruniform gesteckt und nach Böhmen eingeschleust;"alle Welt wußte sich damals, was die Amis in Böhmen zu suchen gehabt hätten, wenn sie sich sowieso gleich wieder zurückzogen.
Im Juli 1954 fuhr ich erst nach Wien und dann nach Klagenfurt in Urlaub, wo ich frühere Kameraden aus dem FlüHi besuchte. Als ich in Wien einem KrimKom. die große Neuigkeit erzählen wollte, winkte der ab und sagte:"Ach das haben wir schon 1943/44 gehabt. Wir bekamen damals eine GKdS in der stand, das und das wird sich in der Luft zeigen, bitte beobachten,Eindrükke hierher mitteilen und zu niemandem sprechen". An einem schönen Juli-Abend hatte ich dann in Klagenfurt meine schönste Sichtung: eine Lichtscheibe größer als der Mond zog mit Schweif von Südwest nach Nordost, am nächsten Tag waren die Zeitungen voll. Da sich zur damaligen Zeit über Österreich diese Dinger massenhaft zeigten, veranstaltete eine Zeitung eine ■■■■■■■■■ und erhielt u.a. einen Leserbrief von einem Dipl.-Ing. aus Baden b/Wien, in dem es hieß:".. jawohl, diese Dinger wurden bei uns im böhmisch-mährischen Raum erzeugt. 1943 wurden die Anlagen auf Befehl des Führers abgebaut und abtransportier und seither fehlt von meinem Freund, der da Einflieger war, jede Spur !!"

He proceeded excitedly to explain to the young lady some of his ideas. He said he hoped for active help and protection from the S.D. (Security Service) in doing experimental work on his project, since both Himmler and Ohlendorf were absent from Berlin at the time, she took the document into safe keeping, storing it in her safe. This document was later handed to Himmler and Ohlendorf. After reading it they contacted aircraft and propulsion experts. A number of top secret conferences were called but with no positive results. The experts scoffed at the revolutionary proposals advanced by the young man, which amongst other things, contained such suggestions as the creation of a vacuum in front of the disc shaped aircraft into which the craft could then move, without effort, at incredible speeds. Also proposed was exploitation of the earth's natural magnetism along with a steering mechanism based on internal polarity shift.

To the young secretary all this seemed very difficult to comprehend and only because it was so totally out of her usual line of work does she remember all of the above details. The closed minds of the consulted experts annoyed her, it was their arrogant **impossible** and **never** which stuck in her mind. Being a convinced National Socialist, she had known of the Fuhrer's abhorrence of the stuffy traditionalists and reactionaries with which Germany, especially, seems to be plaqued? The project was still being discussed when the young man re-appeared, and in a very happy frame of mind asked for the return of the documents. He told our correspondent that he had found someone else to support and finance his research and experiments, even with plant facilities to produce them.

Years later, after the war, when the U.F.O. sightings were the topic of the day, she mentioned the above to a friend, a man, who had been a Kriminal Kommisar (Criminal Commisar similar to the American G man of old) in Austria during the war (then a part of the greater German Reich). He was not at all surprised but on the contrary he remembered having received a top secret telex order, issued by Berlin Headquarters, requesting that the people's reactions to "strange flying objects" be monitored, and that these flying objects would be appearing in the skies over the entire Reich. There would be no need to sound the alarms for they belonged to Germany. The date? 1943-44. In due course, the flying objects appeared. The German fighters thought they were American, the Allies thought they were German secret weapons. The Americans nick-named them appropriately enough, "Kraut meteors". (Keyhoe) There is one final aspect of the lady's letter which seems particularly significant. While in Vienna she saw a letter published in a large daily newspaper by a well-known Diplom Ingenieur from Vienna's fashionable suburb, Baden, and this letter stated:— "We built flying saucers in Bohemia and Sudetenland. My friend was one of the test pilots for these devices. One day in 1943 the entire plant was dismantled and shipped by freight train to destinations unknown. From that day to this, I have never heard from my friend, the test pilot. Incidentally, orders for this dismantling came directly from Adolf Hitler".

A most incredible development. Were the flying saucers not used in combat because the Germans had not come up with the required anti-weapon? Or were they, perhaps, not available because of the rare metal needed in large enough quantities to make the required impact? Or were they used and so devastatingly that no survivors were around to tell the story? Once again, a letter and some suppressed books written by a German engineer, can help us fill the gap. We reproduce excerpts from a letter received by the authors from divided Berlin, Germany. The letterhead of the correspondent states he is a Diplom Ingeneur who seems to head a private space-flight research organisation in Germany and Switzerland. He is the author of several books about spaceflight and we repro-duce the cover of one. The title translated into English is: "German Spaceflight Since 1934", with a sub-title of "A Troublesome Book". In it are many engineer's drawings of weird and strange-looking craft the like of which we have never seen anywhere before. Strange names are given to these contraptions. One model especially merits to be reproduced here for your evaluation. The claim is made that the author launched a rocket to the moon in the early thirties, propelled by a light conversion power plant. In other words, the rocket was propelled by sunlight transformed into energy. Certainly, a revolutionary concept.

In a series of letters we have received, Prof. Dr. Phillips, claims to have been a wartime comrade (W.W.1) of Adolf Hitler, and that they kept in close touch and that Hitler was kept fully informed about all the research and that he, Hitler himself, entrusted Phillips with critical missions, in rare cases. He further states that to this day he has in a bank safety depo-sitory a special pass of the Fuhrer giving him sweeping authority. See photocopy of excerpt of letter.

Two other points mentioned in different letters are rele-vant to our story. Dr. Phillips who speaks several languages, and amongst them Russian, claims to have been employed by the Russians in the very "collecting camps" the Soviets had set up for screening German scientists for use in their own weapons development. His linguistic abilities made him "Chief

57

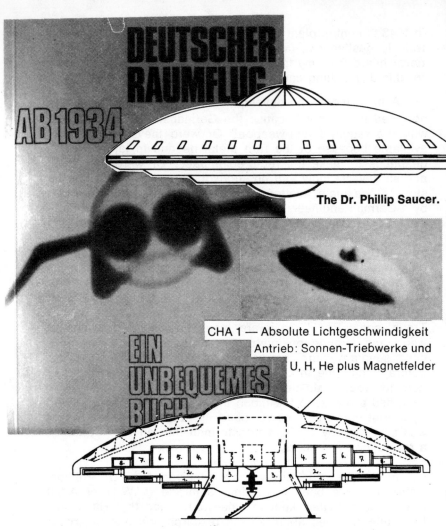

The Dr. Phillip Saucer.

CHA 1 — Absolute Lichtgeschwindigkeit

Antrieb: Sonnen-Triebwerke und

U, H, He plus Magnetfelder

Noch etwas : ich besitze (auch heute noch im Banksafe liegend)
d e n Sonderausweis des Führers über "plein pouvoir" .-

ami-Flieger gültig, die im Rundfunk veraus bekanntgaben : die Bewoh-
ner von Bremen werden ausradiert. Militär war sowieso keines dort !
Nun ruht der Pulk geschlossen in der Nordsee !

Frdl.Grüße
Jhr
(pp. Philipp)

Excerpts of letters

Screener". If all this is true, then one can safely assume that Hitler's friend would find ways and means to ensure that top grade scientists did not fall into the hands of the Soviets at least in this instance. Prof. Dr. Phillips claims he knows exactly who went where and many other details. Dr. Phillips also mentions his experimental work during the war with the practical use of death rays.

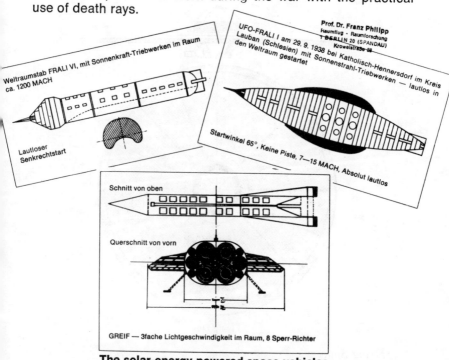

The solar-energy-powered space vehicles

However, there are also other sources available for the U.F.O. verification. There is the best-selling book already in its 5th Edition called "Die Deutschen Geheimwaffen des Zweiten Weltkrieges und ihre Weiterentwicklung" by Rudolf Lusar, published by Lehmann Verlag of Munich, West Germany. A small English edition exists but seemingly is suppressed. One of the authors of this book obtained just one copy from the author himself. The late Rudolf Lusar had been a Luftwaffe Major, an inventor and engineer, he had been employed during W.W. II in the patent and experimental section of the Reichsluftwaffen Ministerium in Berlin. In this book Lusar describes some pretty far-out, highly-advanced technology on rocket torpedoes,

59

submarine fired ballistic missiles, Flying People (see photo) and very detailed information on the flying saucer programme. Shown here are photographs of engineering drawings, top and front view, along with excerpts of his descriptions.

GERMAN SECRET WEAPONS OF SECOND WORLD WAR

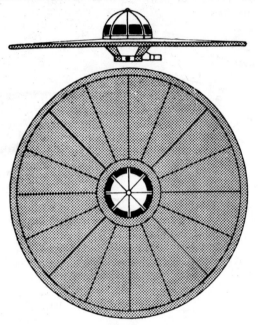

Flying Disc

Flying Saucers

Flying saucers have been whirling round the world since 1947, suddenly turning up here and there, soaring in and darting off again at unprecedented speed with flames encircling the rim of the saucer's disc. They have been located by radar, pursued by fighters and yet nobody has so far succeeded in establishing the existence of such a "flying saucer" or managed to ram or shoot one down. The public, even the experts, are perplexed by an ostensible mystery or a technical miracle. But slowly the truth is coming out that even during the war German research workers and scientists made the first moves in the direction of these "flying saucers". They built and tested such near-miraculous contraptions. Experts and collaborators in this work confirm that the first projects, called "flying discs", were undertaken in 1941. The designs for these "flying discs" were drawn up by the German experts Schriever, Habermohl and Miethe, and the Italian Bellonzo. Habermohl and Schriever chose a wide-surface ring which rotated round a fixed, cupola-shaped cockpit. The ring consisted of adjustable wing-discs which could be brought into appropriate position for the take-off or horizontal flight, respectively. Miethe developed a discus-shaped plate of a diameter of 42 m. in which adjustable jets were inserted. Schriever and Habermohl, who worked in Prague, took off with the first "flying disc" on February 14, 1945. Within three minutes they climbed to an altitude of 12,400 m. and reached a speed of 2,000 km./h. in horizontal flight (!). It was intended ultimately to achieve speeds of 4,000 km./h.

Extensive preliminary tests and research were necessary before construction could be started. Because of the great speed and the extraordinary heat stress, special heat-resisting materials had to be found. The development, which cost millions, was almost completed at the end of the war. The then existing models were destroyed but the plant in Breslau where Miethe worked fell into the hands of the Russians who took all the material and the experts to Siberia, where work on these "flying saucers" is being successfuly continued.

Schriever escaped from Prague in time; Habermohl, however, is probably in the Soviet Union, as nothing is known of his fate. The former designer Miethe is in the United States and, as far as is known, is building "flying saucers" for the United States and Canada at the A. V. Roe works. Years ago, the U.S. Air Force received orders not to fire at "flying saucers". This is an indication of the existence of American "flying saucers" which must not be endangered. The flying shapes so far observed are stated to have diameters of 16, 42, 45 and 75 m. respectively and to reach speeds of up to 7,000 km./h. (?). In 1952 "flying saucers" were definitely established over Korea and Press reports said they were seen also during the NATO manœuvres in Alsace in the autumn of 1954. It can no longer be disputed that "flying saucers" exist. But the fact that their existence is still being denied, particularly in America, because United States developments have not progressed far enough to match the Soviet Union's, gives food for thought. There also seems some hesitation to recognise that these novel "flying saucers" are far superior to conventional aircraft—including modern turbo-jet machines—that they surpass their flying performance, load capacity and manœuvrability and thereby make them obsolete.*

* According to a Washington report at the end of 1955, the United States Air Force was then shortly going to test aircraft models whose appearance would fully correspond to the conception of the "flying saucer". Secretary of the Air Force Donald Quarles has stated that these models are disc-shaped and able to take off vertically. They will do without expensive runways (see "German flying discs").

According to Lusar, of the many scientists who worked on U.F.O. projects only one of these was found, a man named Miethe, and he was from the team who worked outside Prague. His whereabouts and movements are known. He worked in the early fifties for the A. V. Roe Company in Malton, Ontario, a suburb of Toronto, Canada. This man Miethe is the originator of a genuine flying saucer, which was produced by Avro on contract to the U.S. Air Force.

See photograph below — compare similar shape and concept with Lusar's drawings. Of particular interest is the propeller fan blade arrangement. The craft pictured above was shown to the press on the ground only, not in flight. However,

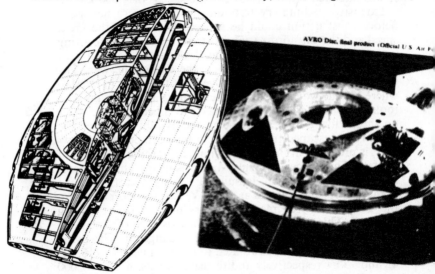

AVRO Disc, final product (Official U S Air F

The much-maligned Avro Disc, built with the collaboration of the German scientist, Miethe. Because it has never been seen "flying" does not mean it has not "flown" when the press were not around. Design clearly employs the "Vertikalzugschraube" experimented with by Miethe and his colleagues in Germany, or at least elements of the idea.

we reprint a photograph or what is purported to be a photograph which originated with the Royal Canadian Airforce in Ottawa, Negative File No. T.P. 1256C, unit 2 Rd. The craft looks similar to the Miethe-designed Avro saucer, that has never been seen air borne by anyone. This was reprinted by the now defunct Toronto Telegram, once the second largest daily newspaper in Toronto.

CANADA

1555-3 (D/Coord)

Commanding Officer
Canadian Forces Photographic Unit
Canadian Forces Base Ottawa
Ottawa, Ontario
K1A OK4

The Truly Great Books
107 King St E
Toronto 110, Ontario

Dear Sir: 25 June, 1974

This is to thank you for your letter dated 12 June, 1974.

Our research department has checked our files and made inquiries at various other photo departments in the Ottawa area, but unfortunately they have been unable to locate the negative that you asked about.

We regret we are unable to assist you with your request, but if we may be of any assistance to you in any future quest, please do not hesitate to write us.

Yours truly,

J.A. Young
Lieutenant Commander
Commanding Officer
Canadian Forces Photographic Unit

The authors contacted the defence department in Ottawa for permission to re-print the photograph. The file was missing and it was reported that no trace could be found of anything, negatives or prints. So that leaves the big question — why didn't Miethe's saucer fly? Or did it fly and we were not told the truth? Or, was Miethe a victim of the previously described German policy of only letting an individual know as much as he needed to know, to fulfill his task? No more and no less! Did he purposely sabotage the American Flying Saucer? Of greater importance, where is Miethe today? I doubt that we will ever know.

The A.V. Roe aircraft company was driven into bankruptcy in 1958-59 by the then Prime Minister of Canada — John Diefenbaker. Thousands of top flight scientists were overnight out of work and the cream of them were quickly hired by Boeing, General Dynamics and others. Miethe and the flying saucer he helped to build have vanished without a trace!

The Soviets too got into the act during the height of the UFO craze in the late 50's and early 60's. Since the Communists have ruled Russia, they have invented everything or re-invented everything, from gunpowder to spaceflight! To assure that credit goes where it is due, reproduced here is the Soviet flying saucer. A poor photograph of a canvas-covered circular-

shaped wingless aircraft, the type the Germans experimented with around 1935 and in concept similar to the United States all-wing bomber. Surely, if the Soviet's had captured, as had been feared for some time, the German UFO teams and their factories, they could have come up with something a little better! And so again, we must conclude there is a missing link.

Where are the flying saucer teams now? Or better still, to where did they go after they left Germany? It is almost a certainty that they did leave Germany. There are a number of possibilities, but all point in the general direction of the Southern Hemisphere.

Essentially, Bar-Zohar corroborates Michael X and Mattern. "The Avengers" page 110 111 Excerpts below.

When the fighting ended in Berlin, some men of the Russian Fifth Army came across a burned-out tank at Spandau, and lying near it was the body of a man wearing a long leather jacket. In one of the jacket pockets they found a small book which turned out to be the diary of Martin Bormann, the Fuehrer's deputy and one of the most astute of the Nazi Party leaders.

The dead man was not Bormann—this was very soon verified—but an entry in the diary, in Bormann's handwriting, said "May 1, attempt to break out."

A telegram that the Reichsleiter had neglected to destroy was found in his office: "April 22, 1945. Agree with proposal of dispersal in southern zone beyond the ocean. Signed, Bormann."

These two sentences clearly conveyed Bormann's intentions to flee to South America and showed that he had begun to put his plans into effect on May 1.

There was Peron, Hitler's admirer, in power in Argentina. It is a well known fact that huge tracts of land had been bought up by Nazi money and interests. An interesting aside is that Germany's top fighter-bomber pilot Hitler's favourite, (Stuka divebomber ace with over 2,500 sorties and over 500 tanks and 140 planes to his credit), Hans Ulrich Rudel, worked on secret aircraft development schemes for Juan Peron after the war. He met Peron personally on several occasions and the team around Rudel, Tank and Horten did produce a very fast jet fighter plane for Argentina. See photographs. From this fact it is possible to deduct that both the facilities as well as the talent were available and did not lay idle. Rudel by the way has made over 75 trips to South America since then!!! What for?

German scientists produced this jet for Peron.

Peron and the German experts

So we have seen Berlin fall. We have looked into the suicide drama, we have seen Hitler leave Berlin for Denmark and Norway. We have double-checked every angle, even Hitler's mind and motivation. We have traced his thinking back to as early as 1920 right up to 1945 and gleaned from his own book "Mein Kampf" and from his various speeches right up to the last days in Berlin and all are valuable insights, having a direct bearing on the solution to the UFO mystery.

Now we must follow the U-Boat convoy that allegedly has Hitler and Eva Braun aboard on its secret underwater journey — to where? Will it be possible to break out of the ring of steel and fire the seemingly all-conquering allies have thrown around the crumbling Third Reich? The first indications come from a captain of the British Navy. His cruiser was part of a large allied force which engaged the Fuhrer's convoy in a battle. The allies were obviously not aware of the significance of this particular convoy, but must logically have expected some isolated break out attempts by a select group of top political and military leaders from fast-sinking Germany. They had thrown up a virtual blockade around the entire North Sea, stretching from the polar region down to the Spanish coast.

The Fuhrer convoy was detected and promptly engaged by all available allied units in the general area, and with unexpected and devastating results. It would seem that the secret weapons, which Goebbels had spoken of in such glowing terms only a few days previous, were now put to use for the first time in an actual battle situation. The result, was one sole survivor from a British destroyer and it was from this, the captain, that the words were uttered: "May God help me, may I never again encounter such a force". The report of the captain's words was carried in El Mercurio, Santiago, Chile and in "Der Weg" a paper published by exiled Germans living in Buenos Aires, Argentina.

Michael X in "We Want you — Hitler is Alive" mentions that the great mediaeval seer and prophet, Nostradamus prophesied Hitler's escape from Germany, and in a submarine, and we quote him as follows:—

"The leader who shall lead an infinite number of people,
Far from their home land to one of strange manners and
    language,
Five thousand in Candia and Thessaly finished,
The **leader escaping, shall be safe in a barn on the sea**".

But there is another verse, even more explicit, mentioning an "iron cage" — a clear reference to a submarine.

Wild beasts for hunger shall swim over the rivers,
Most of the land affected shall be near the Danube
Into an iron cage he shall cause the great one to be drawn
When the child of Germany shall see nothing"

The wild beasts are obviously the raping, all-devouring Allies, fording the Neisse, Elbe, Rhine Moldau, **Danube,** that's where it all ended in April 1945. Or did it?

Michael X also involved Donitz and the German submarine fleet, and speaks of a paradisical oasis in Latin America. There is even more weightier evidence of the submarine escape of Hitler and Eva Braun. On July 10th, 1945 a sensational news report made headlines around the world. (A world that was busy getting ready for the sell-out conference of Potsdam where a final stamp of approval was given to the Bolshevik armies allowing them to rape, plunder and drive from their ancestral homes, millions of Germans beyond the Oder Neisse line, who were now defenceless since the German soldiers, beaten, disarmed and starving were performing unpaid slave labour in England, France and America. The Soviet methods were even more indescribable than those of the rest of the Allies.)

A German submarine, of the latest design, "U-530", had given itself up to the Argentine authorities, but not before all scientific instruments and weapons on board had been destroyed. The U-boat had calmly slipped into the harbour of Rio de la Plata. The Commander's name was Otto Wermoutt. The world was stunned and electrified! What was a German submarine doing all the way down there in South America more than two months after the war had officially ended? Why had they not surrendered earlier?

The U.S. government immediately demanded internment and extradition of the entire crew to the United States. As per usual in Yankee dealings with South America, the colonial master whistled and the Latin dog had to wag its tail. In order to save face the Argentinian authorities "studied" the request just long enough to question the officers and crew about the why and where of their surrender unusual. Since Washington became very insistent, the prisoners were turned over to the U.S. authorities. Special planes had been dispatched to Argentina and the men were shipped off to the United States for interrogations. An icy silence settled over results obtained and also about the whereabout of the crew. Rumours have it that the entire crew answered all questions put to them with similar answers so that the impression remained that they had been prepared for this eventuality.

Apparently little useful information was obtained from officers and crew about the intended purpose and final destination of their U-Boat. However, the Argentinian investigators did find that the U-530 was part of a larger submarine convoy which was travelling entirely underwater and under strict orders to keep absolute radio silence, a measure usually employed only during extremely sensitive and highly-secret missions, for this type of movement risks the loss of cohesion of the convoy and therefore the possible loss of U-Boats and crews to the watchful enemy. Obviously, whoever had planned this mission was willing and capable of losing some boats. The precautions taken in order to safeguard the secret of the final destination are extraordinary.

It was later revealed in a news report that James Forrestal, then U.S. Secretary of the Navy, (who later supposedly jumped to his death from a 13th storey window while in the Walter Reed Army Hospital) had stated that the U-530 was chiefly a transport submarine and had only carried a few torpedoes. They were of a new type called "torpedoes-arana" or "spider torpedoes". In effect, they were wire guided underwater missiles and remote controlled and they never missed their targets. Due to the devastating effectiveness of the secret weapons carried by the convoy, there apparently were few Attack U-boats in the convoy.

Two things, however, aroused the suspicions of the interrogators. The U-530 carried a crew of 54 men aboard. The usual German crew size was only 18 men. There were also unusually large food stocks on board. However, the real surprise was 540 large tin cans or barrels, all hermetically sealed and upon opening were found to contain nothing but cigarettes. This was especially unusual since all crew members turned out to be avowed non-smokers. Now what was a German U-boat of the very latest and very largest design doing, cruising around South American waters two months after the end of the war? And with a triple strength crew; carrying a cargo of nothing but cigarettes?

Photograph of U-530 after surrender in Argentina. Note "tin cans" on submarine — mentioned in text

The average age of those 54 men turned out to be less than 25 years, with the exception of the machinist who was 32 years old. The commander himself was only 25, and the second officer an incredibly 22 years young. (Photograph shows the extreme youth of the crew. Shown with them are the tin cans on the deck of the submarine.)

Faces of crew clearly reveal how young they are. Close up photos for more detail.

Age and name-list of crew of U-530

Officers: Captain Otto Wermoutt (25 Jahre), Karl Felix Schubert (22), Karl Heinz Lenz (22) Petri Leffler (22) Gregor Schluter (32).

Sub-officers: Jürgen Fischer (27), Hans Setli (26), Johannes Wilkens (30), Paul Hahn (45), Georg Rieder (27), Kurt Wirth (24), Heinz Rehm (24), Rudolf Schlicht (26), Rolf Petrasch (26), Ernst Zickler (24), Georg Mittelstaedt (26), Robert Gerlinger (24), Viktor Wojsick (27), Günter Doll (21), Rudolf Bock (22), Werner Ronenhagen (24), Arny Krause (25), Karl Kroupa (25).

Crew members: Herbert Patsnick (22), Sigismund Kolacinsky (22), Friedrich Mürkedick (23), Arthur Jordan (21), Eduard Kaulbach (23), Rudolf Mühlbau (22), Franz Hutter (22), Harry Kolakowsky (21), Franz Rohlenbücher (22), Johannes Oelschlager (20), Willy Schmitz (21), Heins Hoffman (20), Heins Paetzold (21), Gerhard Nellen (20), Ernst Liewald (21), Reinhard Karsten (22), Hans Wolfgang Hoffmann (22), Arthur Engelken (22), Hans Sartel (21), Erhardt Piesnack (21), Joachim Kratzig (20), Erhardt Muth (25), Friedrich Ourez (21), Werner Zerfaz (20), Erhardt Schwan (20), Hugo Traut (20), Engelberg Rogg (20), Franz Jendretzki (23), Georg Wiedemann (21), Günther Fischer (29), Georg Goebl (24).

Extensive checks and cross checks were conducted by the American and the Argentinian authorities with the files at the German Naval Headquarters in Kiel, and another mystery was brought to light — there was no record of a Captain by the name of Otto Wermoutt as commander of U-Boat 530; he along with several others of the U-530 had similar mysteries surrounding them. Interrogation by the allies brought forth from Otto Wermoutt and his crewmembers the same response — "We are alone. We have no living family relations". Apparently, their wives, parents, brothers, sisters and sweethearts had died in air raids or had been killed in some way or another during the war.

Soon the world forgot about U-530 and its fate and was busy listening to radio reports of the sudden arrest of Rear Admiral Karl Donitz, whom Hitler had designated as his successor as military leader of Germany — significantly enough not as the new Fuhrer but as military leader of Germany. Donitz was arrested and with his entire cabinet was shipped off to

Donitz after his "arrest"

Nuremberg for war crimes trials. Germany thus became a country with its entire government behind bars.

In the meantime, Allied Naval Intelligence Units were engaged in endeavouring to locate Hitler's monster submarines which had been built on the insistence of Hitler and whose success once led him to remark "I am of good mind to scrap all surface vessels — the future belongs to the submarine". Not

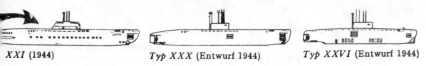
XXI (1944)   Typ XXX (Entwurf 1944)   Typ XXVI (Entwurf 1944)

one single operational submarine was found. It was not until the surrender of Japan that a number were turned over to the Americans. Occasionally, stories were heard of mysterious submarines appearing and disappearing, mostly alleged to be of Soviet origin, or more often, of unknown identity.

On August 17th, 1945, five weeks later, another sensational submarine surrender took place and again at Rio de la Plata. A German U-boat, U-977 under Commander H. Schaffer gave itself up to the Argentinian authorities, and this, three months after the end of the war in Germany. This time the crew consisted of only 32 men, but this was still fourteen above the average crew number. It was soon learned that another 16 men, all of them married and with families in Germany, had been dropped off "on orders", on the Norwegian coast. It would certainly seem that whoever was in charge of this operation was completely in control and knew the smallest detail right down to an individual crew member's family and marital status. From the logs of both submarines, the U-530 and the U-977, it was found that they had left Kristiansund, Norway, on May 2nd, 1945; none other than the exact same spot where earlier reports stated the Fuhrer had been taken after his departure from Berlin.

Photograph of U-977 after surrender

Age and name-list of crew of U-977

Officers: Captain Heinz Schäffer (24), Karl Reiser (22), Albert Kahn (23), ingenier Dietrich Wiese (30).

Sub-officers: Hans Krebs (26), Leo Klinger (28), Erich Dudek (23),

Crew members: Gerhard Meyer (23), Karl Kullack (21), Wilfried Husemann (20), Heinrich Lehmann (21), Rudolf Schöneich (21), Walter Maier (19), Rudolf Neumirther (20), Hans Baumel (21), Hermann Heinz Haupt (21), Hermann Riese (21), Johannes Plontasch (20), Heinz Blasius (21), Alois Kraus (20), Kurt Nittner (21), Heiz Rottger (20), Heldfried Wurker (19), Heinz Waschek (20), Kurt Naschan (20), Gerhard Eofler (19), Harry Hentschel (19), Helmuth Maris (20), Alois Knobloch (19), Karl Homorek (19), Heinz Franke (21), Adwin Baier (19).

The fact that Captain Schaffer had waited another five weeks before giving himself up in the same manner and in exactly the same spot as the U-530 can only mean that he had waited, in the hope that he was to be picked up by a search party. He must have known of the fate of the U-530 since radio reports were regularly monitored. Captain Schaffer wrote a book about his experiences called "U-977" in which he supplies these details. "We were whisked out of Argentina with great haste. However, not before every square inch of the

U-Boat, even floor boards, walls and corners had been painstakingly examined and probed for a trace of the Fuhrer — **In the clear knowledge that the Fuhrer was still alive".**

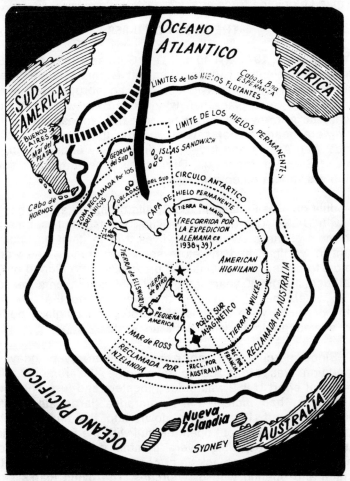

Map taken from the Spanish book "Hitler esta vivo?" — "Is Hitler Alive?", showing the Fuhrer convoy route and the deviation of U-530 and U-977 (broken line)

Less well known, but equally significant, is the report supposedly originating with the British Admiralty. On June 5th, 1945, five weeks before the surrender of the U-530, the 47 crew members of a German submarine had surrendered to the Portuguese authorities, opposite Leixoes, after they had scuttled their heavily damaged submarine. One can certainly assume that this submarine also belonged to the Fuhrer convoy. Time and direction certainly seem to coincide. Perhaps the submarine which had been abandoned had been damaged during the allied blockade force attack?

THE STORY OF U-859

On April 4, 1944 at 4:40 a.m., the German submarine U-859 under Kapitanleutnant Jan Jepsen left Germany for a mysterious mission which was to come to an abrupt end several months later, at a place half way around the world. The unusually large crew of 67 men had not the faintest idea where they were heading. For several months they cruised around Africa then Arabia and India and finally they ended up in the area of Sumatra, Indonesia. During this time they sank some freighters and an Allied troop transport.

Just outside Penang in the Straits of Malakka, fate caught up with U-859. The U-boat was sunk by a British submarine and most of the crew lost their lives. Not in itself an unusual event in wartime, and therefore soon forgotten by the world. Almost forgotten that is. One of the survivor's mentioned on his deathbed, almost 30 years later that U-859 had taken a treasure to its watery bed. He insisted that welded into the bow and holds of U-859 were 33 tons of mercury, all in glass bottles and sealed again in watertight tin crates.

Since mercury is a very expensive item, even today, an expedition was organized to investigate the rumour. After months of effort U-859 was indeed located, and just where the dying sailor had indicated his comrades' large steel coffin would be found. Divers went down into the shark-infested waters and started to cut open the hull with the latest of underwater blow torches. After several months of very difficult work the divers found large black tin crates which were hauled to the surface and opened with blowtorches. The dying man's story was found to be true in every detail. Packed in neat rows, none the worse for their 30 years at bottom of the ocean was 33 tons of mercury.

- Again the question must be asked, what was a German U-boat doing with an incredibly large crew of 67 men, carrying a secret cargo of war-vital mercury half way around the world? To where was the U-boat heading? For whom was the cargo intended? And for what use was the mercury to be put to? Obviously the British did not know the real mission of U-859.

The Mercury Treasure of U-859 after it was salvaged

Here again, was that remarkable loyalty and discipline of the German displayed — this secret had been kept for 30 years, almost unto death. It is interesting to speculate how many more submarines, similar to U-859, were on mysterious missions and to ponder as to where they now may be.

Still more reports of mysterious German U-Boats arriving in South America can be found in "The Avengers", page 105, written by Michael Bar-Zohar, published by Hawthorne Press. Excerpts reproduced here.

Two more U-boats, according to reliable sources, appeared off an uninhabited stretch of the coast of Patagonia between July 23 and 29, 1945. Two sailors from the *Admiral Graf Spee*, Dettelman and Schulz, who were sent to Patagonia by Captain Kay with several of their shipmates, later described their "mission." They were lodged at an *estancia* belonging to a German-owned firm, Lahusen. From there they were taken to a deserted part of the coast and saw two U-boats surface. The *Graf Spee* men went aboard the U-boats and collected some heavy crates which they ferried ashore in rubber dinghies. Then the crates were quickly loaded on eight trucks and taken to the *estancia*, but very soon afterwards the trucks set off again with their load, heading inland. The rubber dinghies also served to bring about eighty people ashore, a number of whom were in civilian clothes. Judging by their manner of giving orders, they were obviously important people. They got quickly into cars waiting for them with engines running, and were driven off.

There has been a great deal of speculation about the size of the Fuhrer convoy. An assumption can be made that it must have been considerable, for otherwise the loss of three boats, with large crews, would have prompted "rescue attempts", an easy enough task in the quiet waters off the South American coasts during that summer season. If Hitler had indeed set up some refuge in South America, we might ask ourselves with how many people. No definite answer can be supplied but again, by deduction, we can arrive at an approximate number.

Perhaps unknown to many north American readers, is the fact that in Europe, there exists a registration obligation for each member of a community. Precise and detailed records are kept of where a person lives, number of children, sex, age etc. and also place of work. Also noted, are details of closest relatives. In Europe, therefore, it is relatively easy to trace and locate anyone and at short notice. True, there was a temporary breakdown in the last few months of the war due to heavy bomb damage and the refugee problem, but conditions soon returned to the usual bureaucratic precision. The Allies found these exact records to be extremely useful in the job of ferreting out "Nazi war criminals". They soon discovered that 250,000 persons had disappeared. Taking into account, casualties and deaths from all causes, this number of 250,000 has remained relatively constant and has been a continual source of speculation. To where could so many people disappear in densely populated Germany? Could the answer be found in a new "Third Reich" located in some far away place? Were select individuals withdrawn, over a long period of time, and re-located somewhere? Were they the "last battalion" to which Adolf Hitler referred several times in his prophetic speeches towards the closing days of the war? Are they the cream of the crop — saved for the day — that inevitable day when east and west shall meet in mortal combat and WE, as Hitler put it in several speeches, "will be the tip of the scale"? Will they hold the balance of power? How? With what? Will their Secret Weapons be the disappeared "Kraut meteors" the "Fliegenden Scheiben" or the flying discs? With what will they be armed? The death rays spoken of by Prof. Dr. Phillips?

ATOMIC BOMB

The great guessing game as to whether Hitler had or did not have the atomic bomb can be answered rather conclusively. The German scientists whom the western Allies scrounged together after V.E. day who were working on the atomic bomb revealed they had reached a critical point in their research. They were part of the teams who had done research work near Berlin and at the Max Plank Institute. Later on they worked at Haigerloch, a little Swabian town in the south of Germany.

The scientists were imprisoned after the war in Farm Hall, an English maximum security prison. Their rooms and cells were bugged with microphones. During the night of Aug. 6th, 1945, when the American A-Bomb was dropped on Hiroshima, the British "listeners" found out how far Hitler's atom bomb had progressed. Apparently it was ready. Prof. Oppenheimer is reported to have said that the bomb dropped on Hiroshima was made in Germany.

Germany first started atomic research when Hitler was sent a letter by Prof. Dr. Harteck. Hitler's order was signed Sept. 26th, 1939. Dr. Esau was put in overall charge. With the capture of Norway there was available to Germany a source of heavy water which had previously been lacking. Production was ordered to be increased by 5,000% at the heavy water plant at Vermork. This plant was the repeated target of frantic Allied bombing raids and a favourite source for "commando raids". Some were very damaging and did hamper Germany's efforts. Apparently one tanker full of heavy water had not been accounted for to this day. It was presumed lost or sunk by a mine. An interesting question would be — "Did it get sent to some place else for later use?"

It is interesting to note that Hitler sent Field Marshall Erhard Milch to the Gottow laboratories near Berlin, where atomic research was also being carried out in 1945, to do an inspection. He also was given wide powers to supply the scientists with anything they might need. During the inspection Milch asked Dr. Werner Heisenberg: "How big would a bomb have to be in order to destroy New York or London?" Heisenberg told the Fuhrer's envoy: "About as big as a pineapple, and we will have a basketful for the Fuhrer by Christmas . . .!" Heisenberg was later tried and the above statements were introduced by the allied prosecutors as evidence!

Two of Hitler's A-Bomb experts. Dr. Wirtz. Dr. Mentz

Hiroshima Bomb — Made in Germany?

Haigerloch Atomic Research

As a passing note, it may be of interest to the reader to know that America's atom bomb effort took 125,000 workers and cost well over two billion dollars. It was later betrayed to the Russians by communist spies.

Was Wernher von Braun and his staff of conventional rocket experts deliberately sacrificed to put America on the obsolete track of wasteful fire-cracker rocketry while the Nazis perfected the superior U.F.O.'s somewhere in South America?

TRUTH STRANGER THAN FICTION?

The following story was made available to the authors by a British businessman who has requested to remain anonymous. The identity of the nurse and hospital are known to him. We include it without commentary.

Letter is unedited. Punctuation and spelling as in original

I have been a night nurse in charge of a terminal geriatric ward for many years and as you can guess have seen some pretty horrible sights, but still met some interesting people, the one who was really fascinating was this German chap I mentioned to you some time ago, the poor chap was a terminal case, a terrible carcinoma of the stomach, he was in a side ward by himself as he rarely got more than a couple of hours sleep a night even with the huge injections of heroin we gave him, but he never complained and was always ready to have a chat, and many a night when it was quiet I would take him in a cup of coffee and sit with him and chat for an hour or so. He spoke English well, with a marvellous German, American accent which he had picked up in America, he had been with us over a year, when one night I was sitting talking about my service in the navy and the conversation got on the Flying Saucers . . . he then went very quiet and gave me an odd look, I laughed and said:

"Do I sound mad talking about Flying Saucers?"

He said no, and then said, I might think he was mad as he had flown in one, anyway I had to leave then but the next night we continued the conversation, for the first time he told me he had been in the Luftwaffe, a security officer, attached to somewhere called Rechlin, where they were experimenting with all manner of almost science Fiction type weapons, he mentioned a wind gun, rockets and laughed and said Germany had all these long before the rest of the world had even thought of them and that given another year or so, the war would have had a completely different ending, and that even now things could still happen engineered by the Reich that could alter the world's future.

I laughed, and he continued, on and on about the progress that had been made during the war years, a lot of things I had heard about but some that seemed way out of this world . . . heat rays, queer new explosives and new type flying vehicles,

79

then he went on about the saucers, how they began with quite small open ones with one man cockpits then on to bigger and bigger ones.

Later they moved to another base, and here for the first time he heard about the so-called "Neuer Deutschland" in the Antarctic, pre-war there had been rumours but never many details, there were many scientists at the new base and flying took place only by night as allied planes were continually flying over, and there were continual attacks, as time went by and the outcome of the war became more apparent the work was speeded up more and more and late in 1943, the first of the big saucers was flying and then came the news that certain specialists were being chosen to go on a special trip to a secret base where the war was to be continued from, he flew in planes on several occasions to bases in the North of Norway, escorting men and women scientists equipment, files, specialised machinery and weapons, all of this was taken direct to long range U-Boats and put straight on board, the weapons were all very modern and he described them as brand new automatic rifles that later were known as MP 44s, there was also a large amount of explosive.

The saucers flew continually and as soon as a new one was built and tested it was loaded with equipment and crewed and when night fell they took off and did not return, as time went by stories of the U-Boats coming and going taking out masses of supplies and people, not just scientific personnel but also administration and military, security, cooks, and amongst them a fair contingent of women.

As the end of the war came near organisation began to break down and supplies ran short they were being bombed and strafed daily by Allied fighter bombers, when the last saucer left, the base was abandoned, he flew on in one of the last planes to leave the base a Heinkel III, they were attacked by a Russian fighter and damaged and landed eventually just outside Oslo. Norway was in chaos at this time but he got a lift in a car with an SS officer, he explained he was heading for a U-Boat base and a possible way out, the SS man had no better ideas and they went North, they reached the base two days later and found two U-Boats refuelling and restocking for their final trips, there were not as many people wishing to use the vessels as most wanted to go home after the war, in fact the cargo carrying boats were even short of crews, they were full of supplies of all sorts, the day after they arrived there was a raid by American bombers a lot of buildings were damaged but the boats were not . . . they sailed that night.

They reached the Antarctic base after a long trip, by sea and across the ice cap, but after a couple of weeks he went back to the coast to carry on his security work with some last minute arrivals on a U-Boat, he then left with instructions to meet another boat in the Atlantic, things however went wrong and his vessel was damaged and sunk by a patrol boat, he was rescued and was made a P.O.W., his captors did not realise who he was as he had got rid of his papers and was wearing naval cold weather gear.

He was held as a P.O.W. in America, and after his release was repatriated to Germany, when he saw the way things were going there under the occupation he got himself some new papers, Polish and managed to get to Britain as a refugee, he settled down, married, his wife died in the late 1950's, and he was having treatment for cancer, radium treatment was tried but slowly things got worse and he was eventually admitted to hospital where he died.

End of letter

Whatever the merits of this dying man's story are, one thing we can be very certain and that is of one terrible weapon at the Fuhrer's command and of which Hitler spoke towards the end of the war when he clearly made reference to the atom bomb — "May the heavens forgive me, if I should reach for that final terrible weapon still at my disposal! We are today already able to blow up half the planet".

Another startling fact proving quite definitely that W.W. II did not end on 8th May, 1945 is the following account in "France Soir", a serious paper (not a scandal sheet):— "Almost 1½ years after cessation of hostilities in Europe, the Islandic Whaler, "Juliana" was stopped by a large German U-boat. The Juliana was in the Antarctic region around Malvinas Islands when a German submarine surfaced and raised the German official naval Flag of Mourning — red with a black edge.

The submarine commander sent out a boarding party, which approached the Juliana in a rubber dinghy, and having boarded the whaler demanded of Capt. Hekla part of his fresh food stocks. The request was made in the definite tone of an order to which resistance would have been unwise. The German officer spoke a correct English and paid for his provisions in U.S. dollars, giving the Captain a bonus of $10 for each member of the Juliana crew. Whilst the food stuffs were being transferred to the submarine, the submarine commander informed Capt. Hekla of the exact location of a large school of whales. Later the Juliana found the school of whales where designated. This is the direct quote from "France Soir". Added to this must be a wire service bulletin releasd by France's own Agence France Press on the 25th Sept. 1946, which further clarifys the above: "The continuous rumours about German U-boat activity in the region of Tierra del Fuego (Feuerland, in German), between the southernmost tip of Latin America and the continent of Antarctica are based on true happenings".

Putting all these details into proper sequence and perspective a clear picture emerges. Selected segments of the Third Reich survived the collapse of Germany proper and obviously did not surrender to the allies as they were supposed to have done under the "Unconditional Surrender" signed by Donitz on behalf of the German people.

There must be rather large secret Nazi bases where work continues on the UFO's and other secret weapons. Investigation shows that huge amounts of money were clandestinely invested by Nazi Front men all over the world, but especially in South America. An incomplete, but nevertheless surprising statistical compilation of these funds appeared in the newspaper "Zig-Zag" in Santiago, Chile, on 19th June, 1947. According to this compilation, Spain received 300 million dollars, Sweden 250 million, Switzerland 100 million and Portugal 50 million and this represents only about 25% of such investments.

This amounts to nearly 3 billion dollars invested in large tracts of remote jungle and pampas real estate, factories, transportation, airlines, shipping(!!!) companies, food processing and agriculture.

In the shockinly candid book entitled "The Avengers" written by Michael Bar-Zohar dealing with Jewish war and post war tactics against the Germans, we find a lot of detailed information about the transfer of German money to foreign lands. Some excerpts are reproduced here.

A most unusual conference of German officials and industrialists was held at the Maison Rouge Hotel in Strasbourg on August 10, 1944. The proceedings of this "Red House" conference are known from the shorthand report, which fell into the hands of the American OSS at the end of the war. A Lieutenant Revesz showed it to Simon Wisenthal, who took a photostat and published it some years later.

Among those present at this conference were representatives of the Ministry of Munitions and the Foreign Office, delegates from the big industrial combines—Krupps, Messerschmitt, Rochling, Goering Werke, Hermannsdorfwerke— and several senior civil servants. The object of the meeting was to decide upon measures for safeguarding the treasury of the Third Reich. They reached two main decisions—some of the riches would be hidden away in the territory of the Reich; and German capital would be sent abroad.

The conference urged that the Nazi Party should go underground in the event of defeat, and should prepare for a return to power with the help of the treasures safely hidden away.

These decisions began to be put into effect in the following months. An "experimental station" was set up near Lake Toplitz and a number of containers packed chiefly with forged pound notes and documents were submerged in the lake, and some other containers were hidden away in old mines in the hills. Most of them were removed again when Allied forces were approaching the region. Although the Allies did not have full knowledge of these hiding places until the report of the "Red House" conference fell into their hands, some information on the Nazis' postwar plans had reached the Allied secret services early in 1945. In March of that year a detailed report on the subject was submitted to the State Department in Washington:

"The Nazi regime has made very precise plans for the perpetuation of its doctrine and domination after the war. Some of these plans are already being put into effect.

"Members of the Nazi Party, German industrialists and Army leaders, realizing that there is no hope of victory, are presently preparing commercial plans for the postwar period, endeavoring to renew connections with industrial circles abroad in the hope of reestablishing prewar cartels. After the war, the intention is for 'front men' to appeal to the courts of various countries against the 'illegal' seizure of German industrial concerns and other German property by the Allies at the outbreak of the war. In the event this method does not succeed, the recovery of the German property would be made through figureheads possessing the requisite citizenship. German attempts to continue to have a share in the control and development of technological progress during the immediate postwar period are reflected in the phenomenal increase in German patents registered in certain foreign countries during the past two years. These registrations reached their peak in 1944. . . .

"German capital and plans for the building of ultramodern technical schools and research laboratories are being offered on very advantageous terms, in view of the fact that the Germans will thereby be able to make and perfect new weapons.

"The German propaganda program is an integral part of this general planning for the postwar period. The immediate aim of this propaganda program will be to bring about a relaxation of Allied controls on the pretext that the Germans should be treated 'honestly.' Later, this program will be extended and intensified with a view to reviving Nazi doctrine and pursuing German ambitions of world domination. Unless these plans are counteracted, they constitute a constant threat to the peace and security of the postwar world."

The American specialists had greatly extended their knowledge of this subject by the end of the war. They soon had a list of 750 firms with head offices in neutral countries, founded or bought with German capital. Switzerland headed the list with 274 firms; then came Portugal with 258, Spain with 112, Argentina with 98, and Turkey with 35. A number of firms had also been acquired in South American countries other than Argentina.

Special accounts in Swiss and Liechtenstein banks were placed at the disposal of the Argentine Government, officially to help their industrial development. Some of the accounts were made personally available to Argentine leaders.

As military defeat and final castastrophe had become more certain, the Nazi chiefs stepped up their preparations for the future—a future in which they meant to have a stake. They had deposited large sums with banks in neutral countries and salted away just as much in the portfolios of apparently respectable persons in Liechtenstein, Portugal, and Patagonia, and had hidden much wealth in the depths of old salt mines in Austria and below the dark water of the Alpine lakes. All of this hidden treasure might indeed permit a revival of Nazism one day—so long as there were still Nazis around able to draw upon it.

Added to this must be the fact that the high priority tasks of the newly elected National Socialist government in 1933, was the securing of adequate food supply for the entire population. Extensive research was immediately launched into areas of artificial food cultivation, in huge greenhouses, with everything grown only on "chemical soil" and under artificial light. Butter was apparently produced from coal and dry milk was another German invention. A method was also discovered to indefinitely preserve wheat flour. Great strides were also made in Freeze Drying all types of food and this was carried out particularly in experimental plants located in the area of Helmstedt. Hitler was keenly interested in these projects visiting them frequently. In a very short time, Germany was more or less self-sufficient and for the first time in centuries. No German ever experienced want and hunger again until the Allies burnt or robbed all the huge warehouses of their contents in 1945 and after.

Any German who lived through that dreadful time will tell you what the humanitarian liberators of Germany doled out as food rations after their victory. In the French zone of occupation it was officially 850 calories a day, in the American zone a little more, whilst the inmates of Hitler's concentration camps, (whose bony corpses you are still seeing daily on T.V. and in the newspapers), received more than double that amount of calories daily. The resultant famine and death from starvation, particularly among the elderly and infants is well remembered by the German population. They call it a "peace crime". The

The victims cf the "Liberators".

food supply for any secret UFO force, (which we shall call by the name Hitler himself had given it) — The Last Battalion, had already been solved. But how about necessary monies to keep such an enterprise running? Hitler had again already planned, with great foresight for this inevitability. In captivity in concentration camps such as Dachau, Buchenwald and Auschwitz, were Europe's best-known and most skilled forgers, — many of them Jews. They were geniuses at their particular craft.

One day, a secret order arrived from Berlin code-named "Operation Bernhard". All the forgery experts were collected and were offered life and freedom if they cooperated in producing for Hitler, perfect forgeries of some of the allied currencies, but in particular, forgeries of the British pound and the American dollar. At first they refused, but one by one they cooperated and in an astonishingly short space of time, they produced what seemed to be perfect forgeries. The German government supplied from its own papermills what is usually the stumbling block to perfect counterfeiting — high quality paper. The plates and paper were perfect, but not satisfied with their own judgement, a secret agent was sent to neutral Switzerland with a suitcase full of "German-made" pounds and dollars as well as other currencies in all denominations. This agent went to one of Switzerland's largest banks and requested to see the manager and stated: "I am negotiating a business deal with a man I suspect of being a Nazi agent, and he intends to pay me in this currency with these bills. Please test them and see if they are genuine". The bank manager explained he could not do this right away since it was in foreign currency, so the Nazi agent left the bills with the bank manager arranging to return within a few days. Upon his return, he was told that the money was genuine, and that the bank would be pleased to accept it for exchange. The agent returned to Germany and the printing presses started rolling in Auschwitz and Buchenwald. Untold millions were printed, so much so that Britain after the war, withdrew from circulation its five pound note — a first in British history.

There is an interesting sequal to this story. Rumours persisted about operation Bernhard long after the end of the war and one such rumour was checked out. For weeks a group of Austrian government frogmen searched Lake Toplitz in Austria. Eventually they found the wreckage of a German plane, the skeleton of the dead pilot still strapped to his seat. In the hold were large metal trunks which, when pried open, revealed over 300,000 British five-pound notes, in neat bundles, perfectly unspoiled and with them, some of the printing plates. The money was confiscated by the Austrian authorities, although it was at that time useless the five pound note having been withdrawn from circulation by the British after the war.

Now remember the U-Boat captain had paid for his food in U.S. dollars and obviously had no shortage of money since each crew member of the whaler had been given a $10 bonus.

It is not generally known that the entire Reichsbank Treasure, (All of Germany's reserves) disappeared from the bank vaults in Berlin, before the end of the war. Guinness "World Records" book lists this story under **"The greatest unsolved robbery!"**

During the U.S. balance of payments crisis, Time magazine carried an article about discussions taking place at the Headquarters of the World Monetary Fund in Basle, Switzerland. They found that 15 Billion Dollars were in circulation, which should not really exist. One wonders where that amount of money came from?

TOP-SECRET NAZI EXPEDITION

Let us now turn our attention to the location of the bases. Again, even in this area Hitler had planned far ahead and at long range. Obviously guided by the possible occupation and subsequent loss of Germany itself, he had cast around for land still available for colonization and found that Antarctica was, at that time, the only continent still unclaimed. With his usual dispatch, a polar expedition was organized, the preparation of which was kept secret. The force consisted of several large vessels, at least two of which were aircraft carriers, not the present-day type but rather large ships with float-equipped airplanes on board. The planes were rocket-catapulted off special ramps at the end of the ships and retrieved out of the water via a crane. This secret Nazi Expeditionary Force was headed by Kapitan Ritscher and took place in 1937-38. The force landed in the area of Queen Maud Land and established bases there. Large float planes of the Dornier-Wal type, with their unusual pusher-puller propellers were used to explore a huge area of Antarctic terrain. Over 11,000 photographs were taken for mapping purposes. Significantly, a Swastika flag was dropped every 20 kilometres to substantiate the German claim to that land, comprising over 600,000 square kilometres in all. In this way, not only was a terrain claimed by Germany, larger than Germany itself, but more significantly, for the first time, ice-free oasis (warm lakes) were found by this secret Nazi expedition. They were photographed along with Alp-like mountain ranges of over 4,000 metres in height. Naturally, the explored areas were given German names and so we have today places like "Ritscher Gipfel" — "Ritscher Peak", named after the leader of the expedition. The hot oasis amongst the eternal ice was called "Schirmacher Seen Platte" — "Schirmacher Lake Group". The different coloured appearances of these inland lakes were caused by alga found floating in the sweet water. The waters are warm enough to allow swimming and bathing with just bathing suits and swim trunks.

The Alp-like mountain range discovered by Germans; the highest peak over 4,000 metres was christened "Ritscher Peak" after the leader of the expedition.

German landing party in rubber dinghy. In background the aircraft-carrying ship "Schwabenland"

Centre: Expedition members showing one of the Swastika flags, dropped by the mapping planes every few miles to underline Germany's claims.

Bottom: German flying boat on the ice-free oasis, warm water lakes, discovered by the expedition. Note pusher-puller propeller arrangement

The German catapultship. One of the large Dornier-Wal flyingboats is just taking off. (Note large motor vessel in drydock area)

The Expedition took over 11,000 photographs, mapping approx. 600,000 square kilometres. Here is a photo of the "Schirmacher Seenplatte" — the ice-free islands, "Re-discovered" by Admiral Byrd ten years later.

The little specks on the ice are seals and sea lions weighing up to 2,000 pounds and "not too bad to eat" and very plentiful.

THE MOUNTAIN RANGES DISCOVERED

Heretofore never published in the English-speaking world, are actual photographs of this Nazi expedition and some of the startling discoveries.

The Alp-like mountain range discovered by Germans;
Taken from the air.

Added credence to the secret bases thesis can be found in remarks attributed to Joachin von Ribbentrop at the outbreak of the war. "In accordance with Germany's long-range political strategy, we have taken into firm possession the Antarctic area, called New Swabia (New Schwabenland) to ensure a safe retreat in case of necessity." (Taken from Mattern's previously quoted German edition of this book).

For an exact location of the German area of Antarctica, please look at the map reproduced here, and compare the relative size of the United States with Antarctica. A huge area, indeed.

Continental United States in comparison with Antarctica

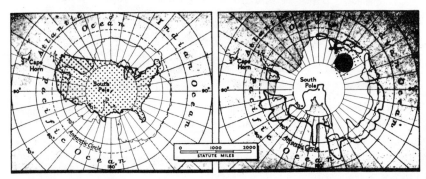

The Byrd expedition and its mapping mission indicated by wavy lines. Black circles indicates German territory. Byrd's intercepted flight marked X

Other factors make Antarctica an ideal place for these bases. There is no rust, no germs, and consequently very little illness or decomposition. Food remains edible forever it seems, since the whole region acts rather like a giant freezer. For instance, the shed where Scott spent some months pre-W.W. I, before he launched his ill-fated antarctic expedition, was recently discovered. The food which remained in the shed, from almost 70 years ago was still as fresh and edible as on the day it arrived in antarctica, and wooden boxes, tin cans, cups, candle and paper (in fact everything), are as well preserved as if by inanimate suspension. Antarctica has no flies, no bugs, — no bacillus can survive the cold temperatures — not even the common cold can survive.

See photographs of Scott's camp.

The camp of Polar-explorer Scott, re-discovered after 60 years. Food supplies which were left were still edible. The table setting was as if just left. No deterioration.

These same non-deteriorating conditions where found in Jan. of 1947 by Admiral Byrd at the headquarters in Antarctica which he had established and lived in for months in the early 30's. From this it would seem safe to assume that human beings too would be subject to the same natural laws and therefore age much less quickly. The significance of all these factors would not have been lost to a very health conscious, vegetarian Adolf Hitler.

Health-conscious Hitler was a vegetarian. Here is a typical meal. No alcohol. No nicotine.

Now could all of this have taken place in the 20th century without detection? Hardly! What steps were taken to discover the truth? What has been done about the secret bases now that their existence has been established and established beyond a doubt? Why did the world not hear about these incredible events?

Obviously, Hitler's escape was soon discovered, otherwise the statements of Stalin and of Eisenhower and all other quoted sources would be an exercise in insanity. It has been speculated that the Nuremberg War Crimes Trials were staged, to a great extent, in the hope that the "Last Battalion" could be drawn from their impregnable, inaccessible hideouts, and thus force the Fuhrer's hand. A large armed force of elite troops surrounded the whole of the Nuremberg area during the long agonizing months of the typically-Bolshevik show trials. Perhaps there are readers who will be able to recall from newspaper pictures or newsreels the "tight security" that existed in the whole of Germany during these trials. Some S.S. men were actually caught, tried and convicted for attempting to free their leaders, but when the orgy of strangulations and torture was

Manned by U. S. troops, an armored truck and a weapons carrier stand guard outside Nurnberg courthouse while verdict is being read.

over, the Fuhrer was still nowhere to be found. Some UFO overflights and activities were reported but no actual armed clashes or incidents took place.

Washington, Moscow and London then decided to really "get into the act"; in fact, eight countries in total decided to do some "scientific" work and in Antarctica, of all places!! A large expedition, lavishly financed was quickly put together. It consisted of over 4,000 specially selected elite U.S. navy troops along with an eight month food supply. Thirteen ships under the overall command of Admiral Byrd made up this purely "scientific" expedition, composed mostly of military-types and very few scientists.

The U.S. Antarctic battle fleet left Norfolk, Va. on Dec. 2, 1946 — three distinct battle groups, comprised of the Mount Olympus, Admiral Byrd's command ship, the ice-breaker, "Northwind", the catapult ship "Pine Island", the destroyer "Brownsen", the aircraft-carrier "Philippines Sea", the U.S. submarine "Sennet" and the two support vessels, "Yankee" and "Merrick", as well as the two tankers "Canisted" and "Capacan", an additional floatplane carrying ship, "Currituck" and the destroyer "Henderson".

At the same time it was announced officially that a similar English-Norwegian force was operating in a support capacity in Antarctic waters around Bahia Marguerite. A Soviet contingent was also reported to be participating in the "research".

U.S. Convoy in Antarctica

The Soviet participation is an interesting one, since Winston Churchill had already spoken of an "Iron Curtain" and felt that "they" — the crusaders to Europe had "killed the wrong pig". Obviously Churchill now realised that they should have destroyed Bolshevik Russia not Germany.

The general public was told that the "RESEARCH" mission was interested in locating uranium and studying the weather. Admiral Byrd, who had already undertaken a similar, though much smaller and speedier, investigation of the north pole was asked why he had recommended the establishment of armed observation camps. His reply, "Because the pole lies between us and our enemies" — El Mercurio, Santiago, Chile, July 7th, 1947. Further questioning as to which enemy he meant, since the Axis powers had just been defeated and had "unconditionally surrendered," brought no response.

However, it was soon learned that as well as the scientific jobs, the mission had the task of "observing the activities of a foreign power in the South Pole Region". Questioned further on this part of the expedition's activities, Adm. Byrd reportedly replied "To break the last desperate resistance of Adolf Hitler, in case we find him in his Neuberchtesgaden inside "New Schwabenland" in the Queen Maud Land region, or to destroy him".

The Spanish book "Hitler esta vivo" page 161, reports that Byrd's expedition was equipped with the very latest devices, amongst them "detectores termo magnetico" — as stated by Ladislao Szabo.

96

The U.S. expedition duly arrived and landed in Antarctica. With them the very latest in military gear and gadgets, from amphibian tanks to troop carriers, helicopters, floatplanes and every other conceivable military apparatus. Bases were established and quickly expanded. Observation planes were sent out all over the region. Reproduced here is a map giving a flight pattern of all the flights undertaken. Many thousands of photographs were taken and mapping missions flown. One particular flight stands out amongst all those reported and one in which Adm. Byrd, himself, was aboard. The instruments went totally haywire and the performance gauges and altimeters behaved in a most erratic manner, causing Adm. Byrd to abort the flight and return to base on "visual" control. All instruments returned to normal as soon as open terrain had been reached.

Attack on base of "Last Battalion"?

U.S. Amphibian landing

It has been reported by papers and sources previously mentioned here, that Admiral Byrd had located the Secret Nazi Base and was approaching it when the above incident took place causing abandonment of the flight, but not before he is reported to have dropped an American flag (some reports mention a bomb) on the approximate spot of the base. Undoubtedly this was done to warn Hitler he was not entirely safe even in his "New Berchtesgaden" or, as one writer calls it, Hitler's Shang-ri-la.

Vengeance was apparently swift and it seems the Fuhrer was not to be humoured. Within 48 hours, four of Byrd's planes had been lost, some without a trace and others without any survivors. (See crash sites marked on map). Adm. Byrd hastily abandoned all his efforts and disembarked, with all his force, for home.

German Base? German defenders? Red Alert!

On board his flagship "Olympus" he gave the following startling interview, translated from the Spanish as it was reported in the paper El Mercurio, Santiago, Chile on March 5, 1947. It appeared on the front page under the headline "On Board the Mount Olympus on the High Seas". Apparently Adm. Byrd granted an interview to Lee van Atta. "Adm. Byrd declared today that it was imperative for the United States to initiate immediate defence measures against hostile regions. The Admiral further stated that he didn't want to frighten anyone unduly but that it was a bitter reality that in case of a new war the continental United States would be attacked by flying objects which could fly from pole to pole at incredible speeds. (Earlier he had recommended defence bases at the North Pole). Admiral Byrd repeated the above points of view, resulting from his personal knowledge gathered both at the north and south poles, before a news conference held for International News Service".

THE NEWARK STAR-LEDGER, FRIDAY, FEBRUARY 20, 1959

Says 'saucers' seen in Far North

By JOHN LESTER
Staff Writer

Unidentified Flying Objects, more commonly known as Flying Saucers, again have been seen "maneuvering and landing" in Northern Alaska and the North Pole area, UFO authority Lee R. Munsick of Morristown told members of the Denville Rotary Club yesterday.

Speaking at a luncheon meeting at the Rockaway River Country Club, Munsick, formerly assistant director of the National Investigations Committee on Aerial Phenomena, told Rotarians

these most recent sightings in the Frozen North took place within, t ebpast two weeks, "as nearly as can be determined at this time."

The Alaskan sighting involved a single disc-type craft that was seen by a small party of trappers about 200 miles east of Umiat, Munsick said.

The men estimated the UFO was about two miles away when they first noticed it, Munsick reported, that it rose and descended to within a few feet of the ground several times, then flew slowly

in a tight circle before disappearing.

They described it as "red colored."

Munsick attributed this to the fact that there are numerous instances on record of UFOs' glowing when in motion, a deep orange at low speeds, nearly white at high speeds.

The Polar sighting was made by two Norwegian soldiers, although no further details are available.

The Norwegian embassy, Munsick said, claimed to have no record of this sighting but added

that all information on UFOs and their sightings were considered classified.

This latest North Pole sighting is at least the fourth in which members of the Norwegian military have figured as far as is known, the speaker said.

In September, 1955, he recalled, a representative of the Norwegian Gneral Staff revealed that "special details" assigned to observe the Arctic region "are now convinced" it was being used as a base by UFOs, especially during bad weather "when we are forced back to our bases."

During this press conference the Admiral also stated that in a quickly shrinking world the United States could no longer derive any sense of security from its isolation or on the geographic distance of the poles or oceans. The Admiral affirmed once again his belief that the entire Antarctic continent should be closely watched and surrounded by a "wall of defence installations, since it represented the last line of defence for AMERICA". (These defence measures have since been taken). Admiral Byrd further stated that no one could give a more accurate accounting of the true significance of the situation than he could, since he had had occasion to employ the latest scientific developments and from what he had learned he could make comparisons. (Meaning he had encountered the effect of the secret weapons?)

When Admiral Byrd had arrived in the United States and the significance of his findings had found their way into the press, he was hospitalized. No hard information was ever unearthed but it seems his frank statements to the press in South America and on board the Olympus were not appreciated by the powers that be in Washington. Was he thus the first victim of a long string of prominent people "removed from circulation" for their honest belief in Unidentified Flying Objects, flying at incredible speeds from pole to pole?

Many definite and also very important conclusions can be drawn from the previous reporting:

1. The final outcome of W.W. II is yet to be decided. This is borne out by the late General and former President Eisenhower's statement—"The second world war has not yet ended" and corroborated by Admiral Byrd's alarming phrase "in the case of a new war". Hitler's Last Battalion is waiting for its golden opportunity to be "the tip of the scale" in any conflagration yet to come.

2. The over forty-four small wars since 1945 including Korea and Vietnam, were supposed to provoke a premature "showing of hands" by the Last Battalion.

3. Hitler has defended his secret lair as successfully against Byrd as he had his numerous headquarters in Europe, during the war against the Allies. Byrd was forced to retreat and to acknowledge the superiority of the UFO's, and their secret weapons.

4. The "New Third Reich" has maintained its crucial time — technology advantage over its W.W. II adversaries — possibly even increased it.

5. Idealism (spirit) has triumphed already over Materialism (money), since only the German state was destroyed but not the ideology of National Socialism.

6. There has been a 30-year cover up by brain and more often by brawn, about the true identity of the UFO's or at least many of them. Their origins have been known, but deliberately suppressed by the rulers of the Unholy Alliance of 1939-45.

7. The real and only reason for the insane UFO cover up, now falling apart, is to be found in most UFO's German origin. The Allies in East and West have told so many lies about the barbaric, sadistic behaviour of the Nazis, that they now fear wide-spread panic amongst their populations, should the truth become known. After all, if the Nazis are still around, would it not be logical and natural for them to take revenge one day? With U.F.O. power!

WHY THE BIG UFO COVER-UP?

For 30 years some of the world's most imaginative people have wondered about the "strange" behaviour of their governments when it came to the questions of the UFO's. If the UFO's are extra terrestrial and the humans on this planet have no "defence" against them, then why annoy these beings by orders to "shoot to kill?" It is interesting that once again we see perfect harmony of approach between the U.S. and the Soviets. Recently there was a very detailed report about the Soviet Air Forces having stumbled upon some secret UFO bases in far off Mongolia. Apparently the Soviets went in in their usual barbaric style, bombed and burned everything to the ground, as reported by Dipl. Ing. A. Schneider in the Viennese newspaper, K. Die aktuelle Serie, P.a. Sat. Sept. 14, 1974.   ". . . the following remarkable report reached us today from the Soviet Union: April 24, 1970 was a day that all hell broke loose. A supersonic Soviet jetbomber in a secret mission from Moscow to Vladivostok was lost without a trace over Siberia. The pilot was in voice contact with ground control stations when suddenly the transmission was interrupted. An intensive search by nearly two hundred planes was quickly organized over the area where the pilot was last heard from. Almost simultaneously a number of pilots reported to ground control "we are not alone up here, above us are flying objects, may be 25 or even more. They are huge, they are so high we cannot get near them". That same afternoon in Krasnojarsk, red alert was sounded and troops were deployed around the city because an entire formation of these silvery, silent visitors circled over the scared town. Apparently, entire salvoes of ground to air missiles were fired at hundreds of flying discs which crowded the airspace of the Sino-Soviet-Mongolian frontier area. There was a concerted action by the strange intruders against the town of Ulan Bator, where all flights seemed to emanate from and end. A spokesman for a group of touring German students said after returning from Mongolia, where they had been at the time of the "UFO invasion", that the Soviet Union had destroyed a secret UFO base of immense proportions consisting of many miles of subterranean tunnels, and dozens of pyramid like structures in the northern area of Mongolia." However no photographic proof or documentary evidence exists. The Soviets are always very secretive.

After Admiral Byrd's hasty retreat from Antarctica he not only suggested bases around both poles and a ring of armed camps, but offered this plan: Turn Antarctica into atomic test ranges where atom and hydrogen bombs could be dropped to be "tested". No sooner had the idea been advanced and announced in the press than a strange thing happened. Capitol Hill in Washington, D.C. received an official visit. There is not a UFO fan who has not seen this historic photograph of an entire "swarm" of U.F.O.'s flying over the nearby Congressional Buildings and the White House in perfect, "typically-

German" formation. Many UFO researchers have been puzzled about that particular flight. Was it a demonstration of strength? Strength calculated to show that open cities such as Washington or New York, with the many skyscrapers, were far more vulnerable to havoc than the continent of Antarctica with its three to four mile thick ice cap. Interesting too, that the Antarctic test site idea was never again seriously considered. Perhaps we should score another victory of the Fuhrer's "Last Battalion"?

Many sightings took place around the world from Japan to Korea, where we have a particularly good example of a UFO de-materialising in front of the cameras. (See photo.) One must ask "Why do these UFO's always show themselves, but why do they not land"? If one accepts the normal theory that they are extra terrestrial then the behaviour is certainly strange. Did the crews of these UFO's travel for so many millions and millions of miles and now not be able to make up their minds to land or not to land? Hardly sensible. Surely it makes more

sense to assume they are from this earth, consequently they don't have to land since they know what earth is all about, and that they are, in fact, reconnaissance aircraft of some earthly power and have no need or desire to communicate. After all, they can tune in and monitor all radio, T.V. and telephone conversations without too much effort, and this would be "old hat" to people who have lived with this, our own technology, all their lives.

A book which makes very interesting reading is "Incident At Kearney" written by a German American who claims, and claims most convincingly, that he was taken up in a UFO on several occasions. He writes that the entire crew spoke German and behaved like German soldiers. He was taken on a flight to the pole. (Why to the Pole and not to the jungles of Africa or Brazil???) They were friendly and correct to him. No sooner had this author, Reinhold Schmidt, landed in his native America than he was put through a regular hell on earth. Soviet methods were used to persuade him to "shut up" including the K.G.B. tactic of "insane asylum" treatment as reported by Solzhenitsyn and others. One further note of interest is that Schmidt was taken up in a UFO which matches exactly the shape and design of at least two German design UFO's. Just coincidence? I am inclined to think not.

The UFO cover up is similar in action to those other unholy alliances such as the mass murders of Operation Keelhaul, at Katyn, Dresden and Hiroshima. Let anyone dare to "not conform" with "the establishment's" version of things and we see people being hounded, defamed and persecuted.

The same pattern that applied in politics globally, when the non-conformist Hitler threatened to upset the international applecart, is still being applied to the UFO cover up and has been applied for the last 30 years. Why?

Finally even N.A.S.A. seems to have caught on that rocketry is a rather old fashioned method of spaceflight and according to "Das Neue Zeitalter", of 5th August, 1967, is now ready to "drop rocketry in favour of flying saucers for flights beyond the Sun and Jupiter". However, not too much has materialized in that direction to this date.

It is here that another question must be asked. At the speed of our own space vehicles, the nearest "base" for visitors would be 170,000 years away. Well, that's quite a distance. Even granting a superior technology which could increase speed ten-fold, it would mean that the saucer crews would have to have taken off 17,000 years ago, when we barely had hairy Neanderthal "ancestors" grunting their way through caves along the "corocodile" invested Rhine. At that time, we had not even invented the wheel, hardly fire, never mind rockets. The only aircraft around at that time on this planet were, at best, birds and may be a few fire-flies. The space people could hardly have been worrying about us and our atomic experimenting — not when they left their bases, so perhaps we should stop making ourselves the laughing stock of the universe. Undoubtedly there is life out there in space amongst all those lovely stars in the sky. Not to believe this would be the height of ignorance and arrogance. Most of the UFO's we are hearing about on this planet are **earthlings!**

In 1959, in three separate large circulation newspapers in Santiago, Chile, it was reported on the front pages that UFO's had been seen, had landed, and that the crew members behaved and talked like "soldados alemanos". When the big UFO flap was on in the Catskills and in New York and in New Jersey in the early sixties, farmers repeatedly spoke of the crew members as addressing them in German or in English with a German accent. The power of the UFO's was pretty well demonstrated beyond the shadow of a doubt by the great "black out". Many people still insist the black out was the work of UFO's. There certainly was a rash of sightings at the time over and along hydro lines and power stations.

Often, UFO fans advanced the theory that the strange flying objects come from distant planets and galaxies to check on our "atomic experimenting", and some people state "contactees" have been told that the UFO's would prevent an atomic war on the planet earth. Why should they? Why should they care? They certainly do not demonstrate any great desire to colonize the earth — at least not in any great numbers. However if they are from earth, this attitude makes sense.

Unknown Object Sighted in Argentina
11/14/64

BUENOS AIRES, Argentina — (Reuters) — Argentine astronomers Sunday were puzzled over a red, unidentified flying object which sped across flattened, and red crossed the observatory's telescope range in four minutes, whereas normal artificial satellites take roughly 18 minutes.

But there are other reasons why the UFO's will not allow atomic devastation to wreck this planet:—

a) The UFO's are, by this time, driven by electro magnetism, consequently all secrets surrounding electric power have been discovered. Since all modern communications and guidance systems are based on electronics, it is an easy task to "listen in", decode and prevent the start or to re-direct whilst in flight, any vehicle or space craft, now in use by the "allies".

b) The destructive power of atomic weapons is therefore much more of a threat to the powers who possess them and have them stored in silos, in subs, in planes or on their own soil than to those countries who do not have these weapons at all, since they could quite easily be set off by remote control from the UFO's, before they were even launched.

c) The UFO's will undoubtedly prevent atomic war to prevent the extinction of the White Race. At the moment the white people are outnumbered ten to one on the planet and should there be an atomic exchange the ratio would be a hundred to one in our **dis**-favour.

No man of the calibre of Adolf Hitler, deeply committed to the survival and resurgence of Western Culture, would ever allow this tragedy to happen to the White race.

There is an interesting aside to this UFO Antarctic business and spaceflight. Perhaps a few of our readers know that in the region of the South Pole (Antarctica), and to a lesser extent the North Pole, it is possible to escape from the earth's magnetic pull and death through radiation because the Van Allen Belts open up, funnel-like, at both of these extremities. It is possible to launch a spacecraft, with very little radiation protection from this area avoiding enormous weight, a crew needs no radiation-protection gear.

105

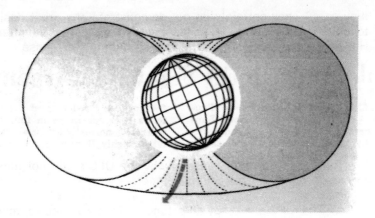

The Van Allen Belts; radio active death belts surrounding the planet earth. They are open funnel-like at the north and south poles, permitting flight into space without heavy lead shields and protective suits.

We must also remember Hitler's feasibility studies of space stations, based on Prof. Dr. Oberth's ideal, 2-hour trajectory. An artificial satellite was to be rocketed into space in 1947 with the A9-A10 rocket, in a steep angle away from the axis of the earth, and counter to the earth's rotation. From this point it would have been possible to:

1) Observe any spot on earth within any given two hour time period.

2) Hit any spot on earth with accurate missiles, bombs, radar-guided or other gadgets such as "mirror beams" or "death rays".

Julius and Ethel Rosenberg mentioned these platforms in their testimony during their espionage trials. They called them "Warships of space". Where did they get this information about these top secret plans, not realised by the Allies until 25 years later? From the same documents that gave them the atomic bomb? But all of this is an indication that spaceflight was already known to a mysterious group of beings.

The American astronomer, Prof. Dr. James Greenacre and four of his colleagues made an astounding observation from Flagstaff, Ariz. Observatory and reported it to a Conference on "Moon Problems" in New York City in May of 1964. Because

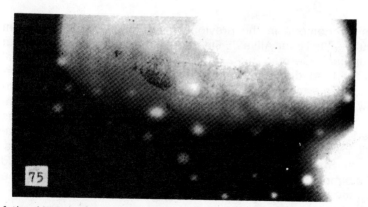

75

of the UFO cover-up policy still in force by the U.S. government, Prof. Dr. Greenacre was only able to give his report verbally to colleagues who were present at the Conference. Here is roughly what he said "On 29th Oct. 1963 we observed several colourful spots on the Moon, the spots moved in formation across the motionless face of the moon. One month later Prof. Dr. Greenacre observed the same phenomena. The May 1966 issue of "UFO Nachrichten" Vol. 117 reproduced what Dr. Greenacre had stated he had observed . . . "Prof. Dr. Greenacre saw on or close to the moon at least 31 space craft of gigantic size. Some were from 300 metre to 4.8 kilometres long. They were in motion while being observed through the telescopes. Also, clearly discernible were numerous smaller craft approximately 150 metres in diameter, which moved past or alongside the huge craft, the "mother craft" occasionally changing colour, as in the often-reported, pulsating style." (The distance from the earth to the moon is 384,000 kilometres). End of report.

The American Professor thought at first the Russians might have beaten the Americans to the punch but as it turns out, the workers' paradise has not managed to land even a man on the moon — last report was that they were seen improving the brand barbed wire used in their more than 1,000 slave labour and death camps on earth, not on the moon. So, who is out there in the wild blue yonder? Prof. Dr. Phillips of Berlin, Hitler's wartime comrade claims he knows! He even sent the author of this book some charts and times tables of his flights. They match!!

Before we leave this area of investigation, we have to look into the repeatedly reported "glowing" or "pulsating" lights emanating from U.F.O.'s. We find an interesting reference to this phenomena in the previously-mentioned book "We want You" — "Is Hitler Alive?". On page 17 the author reports about a brilliant German metallurgist who had created "a metal harder than diamonds" called appropriately enough "Impervium". This metal glows alternately in the colours of the rainbow when heated to a high degree. This seems to tie up another loose end. Again the timing is interesting. The metal was used for the first time commercially in 1935-36. The laboratories were located not at Schramberg as Michael X reports, but at Starnberg and Starnberger See. However, this could be a simple spelling error by someone not too familiar with the German language.

Now it is time for us to get deeper into the state of actual German UFO research and development. Some is based on hard evidence, other areas have to be pieced together from bits and pieces.

German research and science were once the envy of the world. Every time Nobel prizes were awarded, one could find half a dozen Germans amongst those honoured. That was for achievement, real honest effort; recently, the only Germans so honoured were for betraying the interests of their country, usually to the Reds, in the east. When German scientists were given proper encouragement, sufficient funds and lofty goals their creative output was truly amazing. In the few short years from the time Hitler achieved power, the Germans graduated from W.W.I-type airplanes to jets. The first all jet-powered plane was aloft in 1938 — a Heinkel. Since Germany was forbidden by the Treaty of Versailles to build large planes or military planes, research and development was taking place clandestinely in Russia for a time, but Russia being the type of country it was and still is, this work did not amount to very much.

In National Socialist Germany as soon as Hitler gave the directive, things got rolling. A tremendous amount of experimental work was carried out in several fields of development, namely:

a) conventional propeller-driven planes, usually all metal skin.
b) experimental, all-wooden, to scale delta wing airplanes, and all wing designs.
c) jet-powered planes and rockets, as well as turbo props.

108

d) the futuristic designs, such as flying disc and boomerang-type aircraft, powered various ways; flying platforms, people, tanks etc.

e) the helicopter, rotating wing, the gyrocopter designs as well as U-Boat pulled kites and gyroscopes etc.

During peace time all this work was carried out at regular aircraft plants near airports of major aircraft producing towns such as Munich, Augsburg, Stuttgart etc. These places were safe from aerial attack until America got involved in the war.

Then the designs on the more futuristic designs were transferred to Silesia, East Prussia, the Sudetenland, Bohemia etc. The laboratories were usually underground in abandoned salt or coal mines, in some cases, however, entire mountains were honeycombed with a maze of tunnels, shafts, elevators and underground railroads. Smoketacks were camouflaged as medieval castle turrets. Entrances were so well camouflaged by entire forests that had been transplanted and in one such case it took playing youths six weeks after the war to stumble on a secret jetbomber factory the Americans had overlooked.

One case, known to the author's father, is the airfield in the Sudetenland, without any runway. The entire airfield, in effect, was built into a mountain. The planes touched down on what looked like the extension of a regular highway and were immediately gobbled up by a yawning crack in the side of the mountain. On the opposite side of the mountain, the jets would roar out at almost the speed of sound whenever they took off. Eventually, the Allies stationed 20 fighters on an around-the-clock basis always circling the "hole in the ground", hitting the elusive German fighters at that crucial time when forced to slow down to aim for the hole in the mountain. It is in bases like the above-mentioned, that some of the UFO experiments were conducted. All areas were guarded by electrified barbed wire, constant patrols and minefields. It was only possible to enter with special passes granted only by Himmler's Headquarters, all were consecutively numbered and had a picture of the bearer affixed. All security arrangements were in the hands of the S.S. Troops. Often when rumours got around to flying discs, wings etc. amongst these S.S. Troops, they refer= red, in hushed tones to "Himmler's baby", leaning on a play in words, since Himmler in German means sky — "Himmelskind" or "child of the sky or heaven". Why this strange nomenclature? Actually it is not so strange at all. The German "Landser", the popular nickname for the German version of the G.I. had always developed short, but very fitting descriptive titles. For instance, when the Russians introduced their feared rocket batteries which sent a salvo of 12-16 projectiles screaming across to the German lines, it sounded like discordant organ music, therefore it was immediately nicknamed the "Stalinorgan". So to the S.S. men the flying saucers became known as Himmler's babies", just as the Americans quickly called them "Krautmeteors", appropriately enough, since they were fast as meteors and just as silent.

Let us visit one of the German saucer bases as described by the late Prof. Dr. Friedrich Kuhfuss, who died in Barcelona, Spain, in exile, having never been captured by the Allies. Prof. Kuhfuss had for years been involved in all manner of experimental flying activities. His family was wiped out by an American air raid and he vowed he would rather take his knowledge on flying saucers to his grave than to ever share them with "those barbarians from across the seas or those peachy complexioned hypocrites along the River Thames". From Dr. Kuhfuss we at least know how one of these bases looked . . .

BASE X

Deep among the near-primeval, dark and foreboding forests, somewhere in one of the many hilly areas of Germany, there was a secret base simply called X. To the outside world it looked like an ancient hunting lodge, perched atop a small hill. Only two meandering winding roads led up to the "Jagdschloss" as German woodsmen and small farmers of the nearby village (about 8 km. distant) would simply call it. Apparently some gruesome murders had taken place in centuries past at the castle and local woodsmen insisted that on certain nights one could hear the frightful din and clash of arms and the shrieks and cries of the wounded and dying. Therefore the spot was treated with a peasant's healthy respect, for stories of this type were never taken too lightly in Europe. However, someone in high places had apparently not heard of the ghosts and had decided that because of its strategic location at the end of the world, the Jagdschloss would be a good site for some far out experimentation and before the peasants and woodsmen knew what was happening, their forest area had been declared a restricted area. They were told that for the duration of the war the entire area was under the direct control of the S.S. All villagers were issued with special passes, with photographs; no outsiders were allowed to visit them and they were sworn to secrecy. War was war, and this was not the first time in their lives they had had to restrict their lives because of special circumstances and besides they found a ready market amongst the soldiers for some of the few things they had to offer for sale, such as eggs, the occasional chicken, goat, rabbit and perhaps even a pig. They observed, however, bus loads of people driving through their village usually sombre looking men, very few women, but many of them uniformed and an exceptional number of higher rank officers.

Since there was only one Inn in the village, The Gasthaus zum Goldenen Ochsen (The Golden Oxen) occasionally some of the heavy Mercedes and Opel automobiles would stop and their occupants lunch or partake of snacks. The men behaved in a most peculiar manner. They all took their briefcases with them to lunch, many of these cases being of a size larger than the usual German briefcase. They were chained and locked to left wrists and time and time again the local peasantry stood open-mouthed with amazement as these people from "the outside world" descended upon their peaceful Inn, asking for dishes with which they were not familiar and asked for in German dialects which they could hardly understand. However, the hand motions of the eaters, sometimes shooting into the air, or weaving back and forth, sometimes hovering and the occasional word fliegen (flying), schweben (float in air), aufsteigen (climb up) which they could understand, they began to realise that something to do with flying was being discussed and obviously in connection with the Jagdschloss.

One day, one visitor even asked the proprietor's daughter

to fetch some old saucers from the kitchen with which a very serious group of men piled out into the courtyard and watched with much excited discussion and nodding, how saucer after saucer was hurled into the air like today's "Frisbees", to demonstrate to the assembled guests (obviously scientists) the flight peculiarities of Saucers, all of this much to the chagrin of the young woman, because dishes were a pretty precious commodity during war. However, the guests paid well for them, more than the "new" price and after the demonstration they roared out of town.

There was relative quiet for a number of weeks and then one day S.S. men asked the local burgermaster to call together the local inhabitants. An officer was introduced, he announced that close to the Jadgschloss an auxilliary to a concentration camp was to be set up and that the inmates were war plant workers engaged in extremely important work. Nobody was to fraternize with these people and all strangers or strange happenings were to be immediately reported to the S.S. Ortskommandatur. The inhabitants were thanked for the exemplary manner in which they had treated their "uninvited" guests and hoped for future good relations. He raised his arm, everybody said "Heil Hitler" and he walked out, leaving the townspeople talking excitedly amongst themselves. A few days later, truck after truck loaded with construction equipment of every conceivable description rolled through the village. Then followed wood lumber, many rolls of tarpaper and finally barbed wire. Later, followed a few buses, with windows painted over, followed by truckloads of steel-helmeted soldiers with carbines. Quiet settled again on the village. A few weeks later, where there had been meadows was now a hustling, bustling camp.

Soon loud and frightening blasts could be heard day in and day out, reverberating through the valleys. After a few months they ceased. Then huge, slow-moving, flatbed trucks began to arrive carrying loads, covered with tarpaulins all chained to the platforms and guarded by soldiers. This went on for many, many weeks. By now the whole village was rife with the most unbelievable rumours.

One night, the entire village was awakened and terribly frightened by sound of such high pitch and frequency that had commenced only as a hardly audible humming, that it was soon realised that something very unusual was happening. They rushed outside and to their utter amazement and bewilderment they saw a brilliantly illuminated "thing" hovering in the air in the general direction of the Jagdschloss. Then, just as violently as it had announced its arrival the sound died down, the light faded and the strange "thing" settled behind the treetops, out of sight of the relieved, yet still shaken local people. Eventually, this strange sound became familiar to them and only the children became excited about it everytime a "thing" started or landed. Soon, several of these strange vehicles, each a little different from the other, were flying about, at first slowly but later at such fantastic speeds that it was difficult to follow them with the naked eye. But now a new annoyance frightened the farmers. They had observed that their cows and dogs seemed to be affected by the high whine of the engines of these "things". Sometimes, when flying so fast, they made frightful noises, big bangs, that reverberated around the valleys rather like heavy thunderclaps. All in all they were beginning to be a little "unheimlich" (scary) and there was talk of asking the mayor to protest again these shenannigans to the S.S.-Ortskommandantur.

In the meantime, two of the local boys who were in the Army, came home on leave. When they were told what was going on they mentioned to their folks the nicknames "Himmelskinder", and how it was thought that they were the miracle weapons the Fuhrer had spoken of several times in the last few months. This consoled the local population for after all reports from the front were none too rosy and if their valley could help to turn the tide of events and be of aid to the Fuhrer then it was alright with them. So, the months became years, then one day long columns of trucks clogged the roads. Since there were two roads into and out of the Jagdschloss it was difficult to know what was transpiring, but soon they knew. Les and less flying "things" were seen and soon the camp was only a shadow of its former self. One day all work ceased, tremendous explosions ripped, once again, through the valley, smoke rose from the area of the Jogdschloss and a few weeks later the Russians rode into town, unopposed, raping and looting everything in sight. They found only ruins at the Jagdschloss. When they were told, during interrogation, what had been seen, they just stared over their vodka bottles disbelieving the Germankis. Little did they realise that in those caved-in caverns, with electrical cables and wires dangling from now damp ceilings, on the debris-littered floors, in seemingly endless halls, with strange burn marks on the concrete floors, walls and ceilings, had taken place one of the wonders of the world. Now all lay wrecked and mute, only worthless bits of pieces of metal, nuts, bolts, steel rods, rubber tires, some leather and some strange-looking and feeling "slacklike", greyish substance was to be found amongst all the rubble. There was the usual amount of rusty and burnt bunk bends, with their half-rotten straw sacks, broken down tarpaper shacks, half burned, empty cans, containers, some empty munition boxes, guard huts and two or three abandoned, cannibalized trucks. And that was all. No records, no evidence, only destruction.

THE U.F.O. PUZZLE

Technical Details

One could safely state without fear of contradiction, that the UFO origins and their technical aspects, such as method of propulsion, guidance, metallurgical composition of the craft themselves, and the origins of the crews, human or non-human, have perplexed an entire generation of people.

Much has been stated in this book that has never been looked at before in the light of German operated UFO's. Now it is time to look at the available data, real hard facts.

Most people interested in the UFO phenomenon know the Reinhold Schmidt story, so we will only summarize here that he was an American, born in America, but who could still speak some German which his parents had taught him. He has stated that he was taken into a flying saucer on several occasions and actually taken for rides as far away as the poles. The crew spoke German and behaved like German soldiers. Certainly a remarkable story. The crew leader claimed he was from another

THE REINHOLD
SCHMIDT STORY . . .

"My Contact with the
Space People"

A TRUE ACCOUNT OF
EXPERIENCES WITH PEOPLE FROM
ANOTHER PLANET

Photograph of Reinhold Schmidt and front cover of his book

planet, which could certainly be true, and it could mean that Germans have inhabited other planets. Then comes the obvious question — how did Germans get to other planets? Reinhold Schmidt forgot to ask. However, we do have a sketch of the flying saucer he was taken up in, and it certainly resembles the German UFO's that follow, a photo of Schmidt's saucer and the Bellonzo-Schriever-MietheModel which actually flew. There are two authorities who can vouch for the actual flights and some of the details as to propulsion, size, speeds reached in actual flight etc. One is the late Major Rudolf Lusar, author, and an engineer by profession who worked for the German Air Force Ministry and in the patent and discovery evaluation section during the war. We reprint his account of the Flying Disc experiments from his definitive work on German Secret Weapons of W.W.II, pages 165 and 166 of the English edition, published by Neville Spearman, London, England.

Mentioned in other pages of this book

There are a number of speculations which Lusar makes as to the postwar whereabouts of some of the scientists and their plants, equipment etc. which have since been established to be erroneous. However, in 1953 when he wrote this book, that was all that was then known and all that could be surmised. In conversations with the author just before his death, Lusar mentioned that he was going to update the 6th German Edition; his premature death prevented such updating.

Now we must turn our attention to another man who has been closely linked with the German UFO story — Victor Schauberger. Reproduced here are photos of two of his electro-magnetically powered "Flying Hats" and some photographs that show how strikingly similar they are to actual UFO's photographed flying over the United States. Victor Schauberger lived for some years in the United States after the war where he was reported to be working on UFO projects. Apparently he was well financed and supported by a group of mysterious, but obviously wealthy people. He received wide publicity in the middle 1950's when he first published his work on "implosion" instead of "explosion", which is a concept as revolutionary as saying "not nuclear fission but nuclear fusion" is the way of the future. His articles were greatly discussed and then one day in Chicago he just vanished. His battered body was found and as to who killed Schauberger or why has never been solved. One version has it that gangsters tried to beat his revolutionising secrets out of him and accidentally killed him. However, Schauberger did experiments early in 1940-41 in Vienna and his 10 foot diameter models were so successful that on the very first tests they took off vertically at such surpriing speeds that one model shot through the 24 foot high hangar ceiling, damaging not only the roof but also causing the first UFO casualty, namely itself, for it was blown to bits. After this "success" Schauberger's experiments received "Vordringlichkeitsstufe" — high priority and he was given adequate funds and facilities as well as help. His aides included Czechoslovakian engineers who worked at the concentration camp af Mauthausen on some parts of the Schauberger flying saucers. It is largely through these people that the story leaked out.

These are the famous smokeless, soundless, Schauberger Models. Note similarity to real U.F.O. shown in Photos

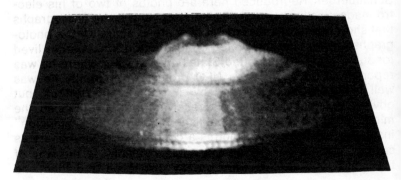

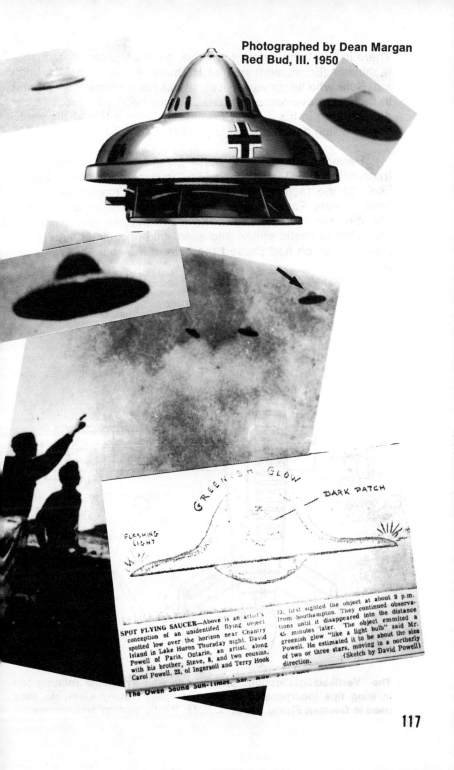

Photographed by Dean Margan
Red Bud, Ill. 1950

GREENISH GLOW

DARK PATCH

FLASHING LIGHT

SPOT FLYING SAUCER—Above is an artist's conception of an unidentifed flying object spotted low over the horizon near Chantry Island in Lake Huron Thursday night. David Powell of Paris, Ontario, an artist, along with his brother, Steve, 8, and two cousins, Carol Powell, 23, of Ingersoll and Terry Hook 13, first sighted the object at about 9 p.m. from Southampton. They continued observations until it disappeared into the distance 45 minutes later. The object emmited a greenish glow "like a light bulb" said Mr. Powell. He estimated it to be about the size of two or three stars, moving in a northerly direction.   (Sketch by David Powell)

The Owen Sound Sun-Times. Sat.

117

There is a further witness to all this, he is a Diplom-Wirtschafts-fachmann (Economist) named Hermann Klass from Muhlheim a.d. Ruhr who wrote extensively about his wartime involvement in the UFO development in the "Bergische Wochenpost" a regional paper in his area. We reproduce here a few of his photo copies which date back as far as 1941.

Hermann Klaas knew Victor Schauberger personally and transported U.F.O. parts from Mauthausen to Vienna and most likely to the factory named Kertl which is mentioned in the book "Flying Saucers over South Africa" written by Sievers. The director of this Viennese firm complained once to Klass about the fantastic speed and silent take-off of Schauberger's invention which had caused the hole in the roof — earlier reported.

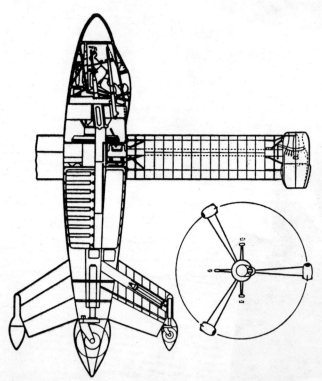

The "Vertikalzugschraube" principle as well as tiltable rotating jets in wing tips incorporated in unusual "plan". Many elements were used in German Flying Saucers. Note: Pilot's seating arrangement.

Let us now examine each saucer in detail. We leave the original German descriptions and add English translations on the engineering drawings.

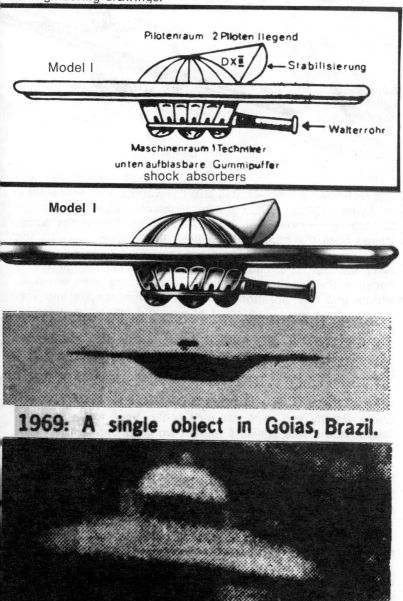

Model I

Pilotenraum 2 Piloten liegend

DX ⫶ — Stabilisierung

Walterrohr

Maschinenraum 1 Techniker

unten aufblasbare Gummipuffer
shock absorbers

Model I

1969: A single object in Goias, Brazil.

1973: In the Rimac valley near Lima, Peru.

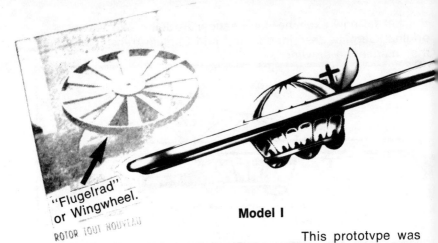

"Flugelrad" or Wingwheel.

ROTOR TOUT NOUVEAU

Model I

This prototype was first test-flown in 1941-42; it is also the world's first vertical take-off flying vehicle. It has similar flight characteristics as the Schauberger models but it was less stable. The wings which issued from the centre of the craft like spokes towards the outer rim, were tiltable. The Germans called that "Flugelrad" or Wingwheel. This caused the designers immense problems because the smallest imbalance caused the wingwheel to vibrate and this vibration increased at high speeds and was the cause on many occasions of wrecked machines. Perhaps the best comparison is to the tire of a car that is not properly balanced or is unevenly worn. Since the r.p.m.'s were so utterly fantastic, the problems faced by the designers can be easily appreciated even by the layman. Whilst car wheel balancing can be corrected by adding lead slugs to the rims of the wheels, German UFO scientists could employ no such crude remedy and so it was repeatedly "back to the drawing board" and it was absolute perfect workmanship which finally eradicated the problem. This model was test-flown with the standard German Rocketmotor then in use and called the Walterrohr. Because of its tremendous speeds, fuel consumption was very high and there was not sufficient tank space on board. At first, the pilot sat in a reclining contour seat as in an airplane. Later the position was changed to lying flat. Provision was made for one flight mechanic whose compartment can be seen below the "Flugelrad". The jet engines on all conventionally propelled flying saucers were manouverable or tiltable in order to achieve what is called the "Coandaeffeckt" which results in the vertical take-off of the craft. Many improvements were naturally made in the course of the experiments and flight trials.

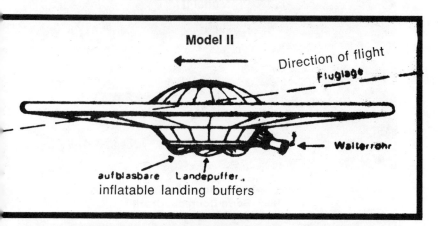

Model II

Direction of flight

Fluglage

Walterrohr

aufblasbare Landepuffer

inflatable landing buffers

Model II

These photographs are identical to the German craft, even including the "inflatable" airbags or cushions that were lowered when coming in for a landing (photos from Australia)

Another U.F.O., closely resembling the German type.

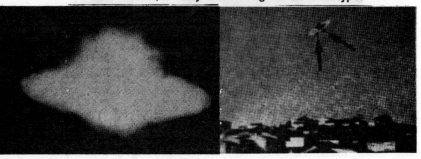

German spacecraft?

Model II

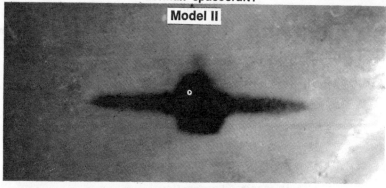

**Photographed by José Martinez Carrasco
June 1969. Serra Dourada, Brazil**

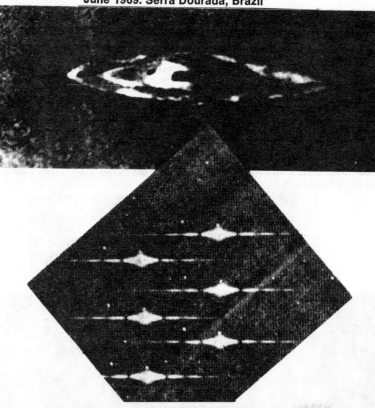

This picture of six flying objects was taken near Vienna
in Austria. T he National Aeronautics and Space Administration said: "We have no conception of what the
phenomenon is."

Model II

GIANT PRINTS PRESSED INTO EARTH AT
CENE WHERE BOY CLAIMS SAUCER LANDED

e Galt Saucer of
ly 30th, 1957

Jack Stephens (centre) who says he watched a round silver-covered object hover for 40 minutes before landing, shows a sketch of what he saw to chums Jerry Pawelko (left) and Danny Oliver. He said the saucer was about 35 feet in diameter and had a turret and portholes.

123

Model II embodies some of these changes. The size has been increased to accomodate two pilots lying in a prone position and the engine compartment as well as fuel carrying capacity have been increased. This model also used an airplane-like rudder steering-assist mechanism for stabilization. Speeds of between 1000-2000 km/hour were reportedly achieved. The problem of wheel balancing had been solved and the wingscrew or wing propeller arrangement worked to satisfaction. The German terms coined at the time were "Vertikalzugschraube" or vertical pull propeller. As soon as the desired height was reached the propeller blades were adjusted to a very flat angle and now the pull up propeller became the "Tragschraube" or carrying propeller — very similar to the principle of the helicopter.

Mentioned in other pages of this book

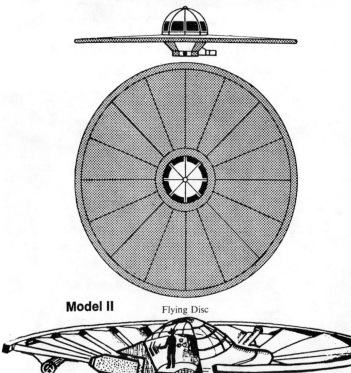

Model II   Flying Disc

Fred Regan's description of the saucer he claims to have been in is very similar to a design by Schriever.

Model III

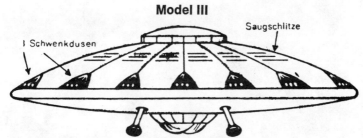

I Schwenkdusen   Saugschlitze

Ballenzo – Schriever – Miethe – Diskus"
Start- und Landebeine, unten aufblasbare
Gummipuffer, ein- und ausfahrbar

Model III

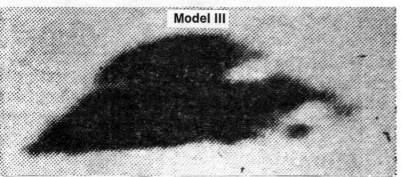

1951: Over a mountain near Riverside, Calif.

Saucer over Rouen, France

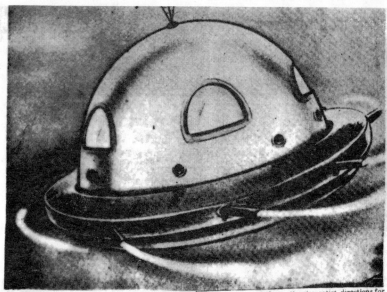

THIS IS IT A sketch of a flying saucer which Herbert Long of Kutztown, Pa., contends he saw on road about 30 feet from his car. He's shown (right, below) giving Leroy Gensler, artist, directions for sketch. Air Guard officers in Reading discount recent saucer sightings in that area. (AP Wirephotos)

'Saucer' in Front of Car

Special to The Inquirer

READING, Aug. 16 — Herbert Long, 39, a Kutztown insurance salesman, reported seeing a flying saucer last night 30 feet in front of his automobile off the Allentown pike near Maxatawny.

Long, an Army Medical Corps veteran of the Second World War, said he was "too scared" to make an approach it any closer.

In reporting his experience to friends here today, Long said he saw a large saucer-like object that appeared in front of his car about a mile off the Allentown pike of macadam road near Maxatawny.

It remained motionless above the earth for five minutes, he said, then "taking off slowly it swished skyward with a tremendous burst of speed."

SIGHTED BY 2 GIRLS

Two Kutztown girls, Carol Hauch, 15, and Mary Kerr, 17, also saw a flying saucer yesterday. Before the object took off, they said, about 1 P. M. in the same county at that seen by Long. They said they told no one about it at the time because they were afraid no one would believe them.

The object remained in sight seven, and two minutes, the girls said. They described it as a flattened sphere aluminum in color, which remained in same while it hovered several hundred feet above the ground, and "Whoosh!" when it disappeared.

'TRAY WITH A COVER'

The Berks county man described the object as being 25 feet in diameter resembling a large serving tray with a cover.

The saucer-like object also contained windows and portholes in the center of the saucer, he said. Long observed "some signs of movement" within the object, and there appeared to be an antenna-like object extending from the top of the dome or crown of the saucer.

He said there was ...

TURNING OUT SKETCH OF A "SAUCER"

Model III

The previous few pages and some of the following ones show quite clearly the trend in U.F.O. development. Significantly some of the best photos, originated in South America and Europe. They span over 30 years.

Illuminated cupola of German Model II or III?

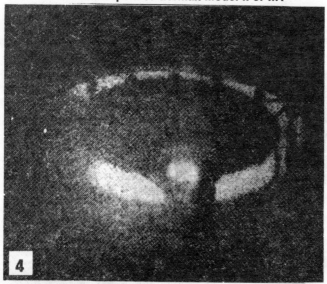

This disc-like craft was photographed over Alberton, South Australia. Experts say it could not be an aircraft or a satelite.

"Sightings" Boom in Mexico

A REAL FLYING SAUCER, at least that's the claim, shows clearly in this photograph taken by a businessman during an otherwise routine trip in Northern Mexico. It was one of dozens of such sightings during a 2-month period.

Photographed by Henk Beverloo, 5th April, 1959. Rotterdam

Model III last known German prototype

Model III This is the final model; some experts refer to it as the Bellonzo-Schriever-Miethe Diskus. This version was produced in various sizes, some as large as 135 feet and even 225 feet in diameter. Actual speeds recorded were over 2000 km/hour. Conventional rocket motor speeds of up to 4000 km/hour were anticipated. As is clearly visible, this model already incorporated a very aerodynamic shape and for the first time also had retractable stilt-like shock absorbers. The craft is ringed by a sophisticated arrangement of tiltable directional jets which guaranteed not only a tremendously increased manoeuverability but also increased speed and better fuel utilization. The top of the craft was ringed by suction openings which had a dual purpose; a) to cool the engine and b) to create a near vacuum into which the craft could glide or ascend into with much less effort. The flight mechanic or flight technicians' compartment was retractable during high speed flying and was only lowered during slow flying or upon landing.

In this advanced, conventional, design can clearly be seen all the basic ingredients of just about every subsequent UFO type which has been sighted and photographed around the world. Undoubtedly, these models were also powered by Viktor Schauberger's flameless and smokeless implosion motors. However, to date, no German technicians who ever worked on these advanced machines have volunteered their knowledge.

We reproduce here many photographs and drawings of UFO vehicles which have been sighted and photographed and any interested UFO investogator can readily compare them with the Model III German flying saucer.

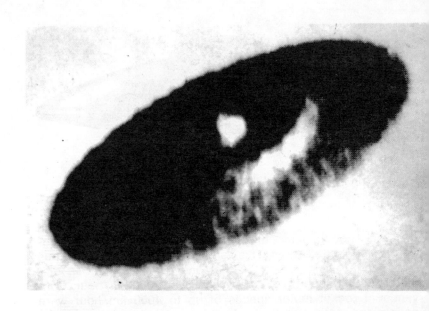

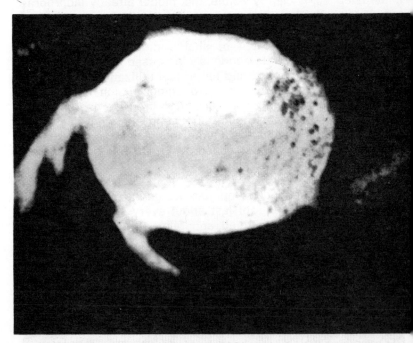

Photographed by Enrique Hausemann-Muller, April 24th, 1950. Spain "Wirbelrad" effect; caused by jet emissions on outer rim, clearly visible.

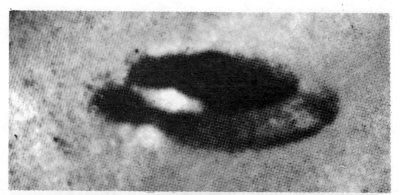

Rouen, France

Pescara, Italy. 1957

131

These four photographs by Almiro Barauna, Jan. 16th, 1958. Island of Trinidade, Brazil.

Sub-U.F.O. surfacing near pole.

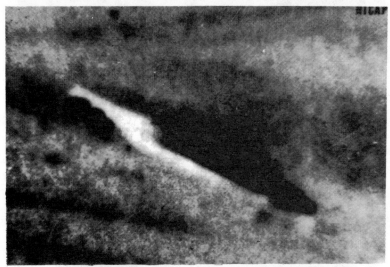

NICAP Photo of U.F.O. observing jet test flight

Photographed by Gunther Wildemann, 23rd November, 1966.
Benidorm, Spain.

G. MONGUZZI Engineer
from MONZA / MILANO Italia
on BERNINA Glacier

Photographed by Dick Blevens, August 30th, 1964. Seville, Ohio

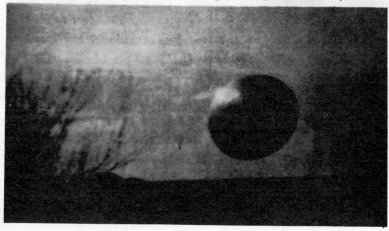

Copyrighted coloured postcard of these photographs available from:
Ventla Verlag, Postfach 17185
Wiesbaden, Schierstein, Germany

136

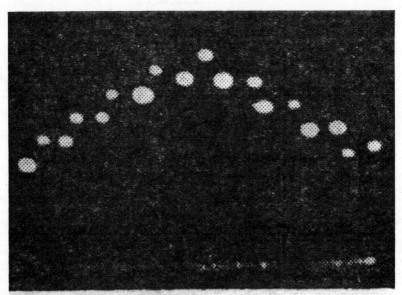

1951: Formation flight over Lubbock, Tex.

Photographed by Paul Paulin, 29th Dec. 1953. Paris, France

137

FOR EARLY WARNING IN DEFENSE OF THE NORTH AMERICAN CONTINENT

MERINT
RADIOTELEGRAPH PROCEDURE

1. WHAT TO REPORT

Report immediately all airborne and waterborne objects which appear to be HOSTILE, SUSPICIOUS or are UNIDENTIFIED.

Surface warships positively identified as not U. S. or Canadian

Guided Missiles

Aircraft or contrails which appear to be directed against the United States, Canada, their territories or possessions

Submarines

Unidentified Flying Objects

2. SEND TO ANY

United States Naval Radio Station
Canadian Naval Radio Station
United States Coast Guard Radio Station
United States Commercial Radiotelegraph Station
Canadian Department of Transport Coastal Station

Receiving station will relay to military destination

3. HOW TO SEND

- MERINT MERINT MERINT (Coastal Station) DE (Own Signal Letters) K (Own Signal Letters) DE (Coastal Station) K
  EMERGENCY (For U. S. or Canadian Naval or Coast Guard Radio Stations)   or
  RAPID US GOVT COLLECT (For U. S. Commercial Coastal Stations)   or
  RUSH COLLECT (For Canadian Dept of Transport Coastal Stations)

4. SEND TO ONE DESTINATION

ComAsDeForLant Norva
ComWestSeaFron Navy SFran
NavyCharge Halifax
NavyCharge Esquimalt

Select destination nearest to your receiving station

5. SEND THIS KIND OF MESSAGE

Content—	Example—
a. Begin your message with the word "MERINT"	MERINT
b. Give the reporting ship's name and signal letters	SS TOLOA WHDR
c. Describe briefly the objects sighted	TWO UNIDENTIFIED SURFACED SUBMARINES
d. Give ship's position when objects are sighted, also TIME and DATE	5034N 4012W 071430 GMT
e. If objects are airborne, estimate altitude as "low", "medium", "high"	(not applicable)
f. Give direction of travel of sighted objects	HEADING 270 DEGREES
g. Estimate and give speed of sighted objects	15 KNOTS
h. Describe condition of sea and weather	SEA CALM
i. Give other significant information	ELONGATED CONNING TOWERS

6. SEND IMMEDIATELY

a. DO NOT DELAY YOUR REPORT DUE TO LACK OF INFORMATION
b. EVERY EFFORT SHOULD BE MADE TO OBTAIN ACKNOWLEDGMENT FROM RECEIVING STATION THAT MESSAGE HAS BEEN RECEIVED.

- The International urgency signal (XXX XXX XXX) may be used as an alternate to clear circuit.

Authorised by Secretary of the Navy

OPNAV 94-P-3B
0420 062 0000

Posters put out by United States Government, Secretary of the Navy, about U.F.O. reporting procedure.

Stephen Derbyshire, England

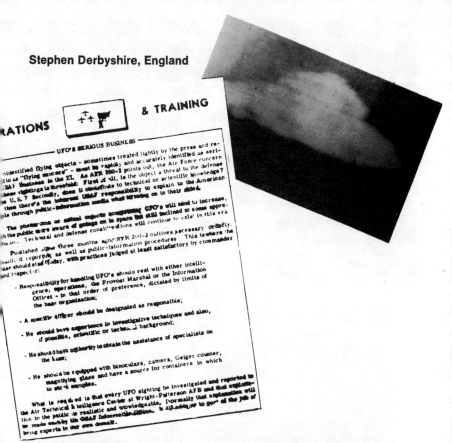

Official U.S. Government poster, recognizing existence of U.F.O.'s and detailed instructions of what to do in case of their appearance.

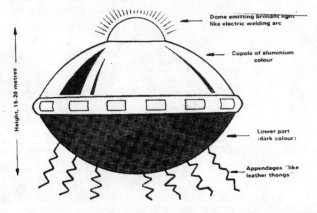

Dome emitting brilliant light like electric welding arc

Cupola of aluminium colour

Height, 15-20 metres

Lower part (dark colour)

Appendages "like leather thongs"

Frequently reported shapes of U.F.O.'s and how they function.

German U.F.O. Base? Flight Control Area?

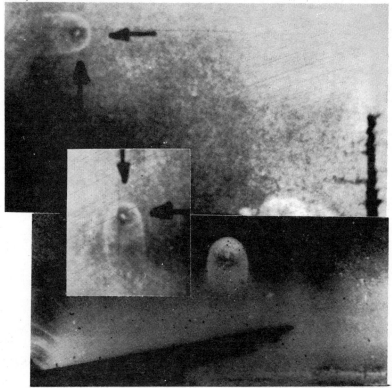

U.F.O. in flight over Washington State 1950. Note identical shape as U.F.O. photographed by German W.W. II Focke Wulf fighter pilot in 1943-44.

U.F.O. formation photographed June 24th, 1965 on World U.F.O. Day, Hokkaido, Japan

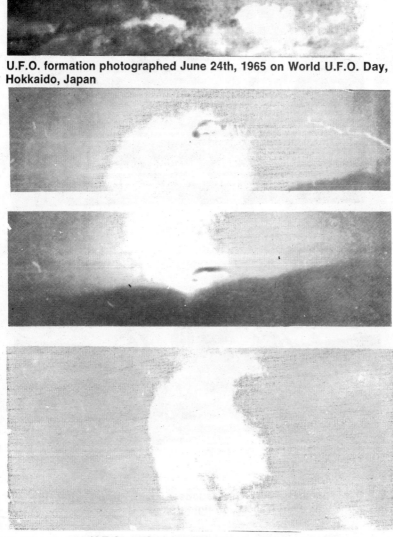

U.F.O. performing like the one at left.

U.F.O.'s appearing over the Japanese battle fronts after the war in Europe was over. Called Foo-fighters!

Undoubtedly, tremendous advances must have been made on these flying machines by those who knew the secret of flying saucers, and any unbiased reader must admit that the German Flying Saucer development ushered in a new age in travel. However, because of the new technology we have to ask ourselves some very searching questions.

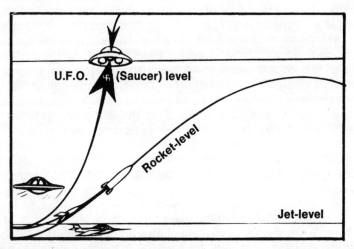

Did the Germans have help from "real" U.F.O. people because their technology was the most advanced?

Did Hitler's scientists perform their "miracle" alone, unaided or did flying saucer "people", perhaps visitors from other galaxies give them a helping hand because they had mastered the new technology and consequently spoke the same or at least similar technological language? Could this be possible? Another question could be, did the Nazis discover some long-hidden deep secrets during their lengthy and exhaustive expeditions to the Himalayas and ancient Tibet? Intriguing and fascinating volumes have been written about these mysterious activities which had the active support and blessing of men such as Heinrich Himmler. It has been reported that the S.S. had an extremely large collection of occult books and medieval transcripts of alchemy and sorcery. Apparently over 20,000 volumes were, at one time, housed at the Ordensburg, Sonthofen, in Bavaria.

Perhaps there are elements of truth from all these stories. Did the Nazis establish secret bases in Antarctica? Did they perfect there a far-advanced flying saucer programme? Did they accidentally discover during their many expeditions that there is indeed an "Inner Earth"? (Nordic legends and Sagas have long recounted very inspiring tales of a perfect society of blue-eyed, blond Germanic giants who dwell in the inner earth). Was the world not astounded when it became known in 1945 that many of the Nazi leaders had been early members — 1918-20 — of the Secret Order of Thule!? It is known that Dietrich Eckhardt, Hitler's brilliant poet friend, had introduced him to this organization in Munich. The great expounder and father of geo-politics, Haushofer, friend and mentor of Rudolf Hess (Hitler's comrade and cell mate of Landsberg) Hess himself and Hitler were all steeped in the ancient mysteries of the Nordic world. It is therefore quite conceivable that the Nazis were the outer earth representatives of the "inner earth" or "outer space" blond, blue-eyed giants who spook through Nordic, Inca, Aztec and even North American Indian legends.

Perhaps Erich von Danniken has uncovered the tips of an iceberg? Are we about to have shattered our comfortable world picture that God created the earth in 7 days etc. etc. And so, again and again we have to come back to the same questions which can only be answered by the same answers. Every government on earth seems to be frantically engaged in suppressing the UFO story. Films are confiscated, pilots instructed to intercept and shoot to kill UFO's. People are railroaded into hospitals and eventually insane asylums because they have seen or even been contacted by UFO's. Why? Why? Why, the UFO crews themselves give most of the answers to the questions. If they were from other planets and had come here to investigate or make contact with earthlings, they would hardly waste their precious time and tremendous expense and effort just to fly around and treat us to pulsating lights in some remote swamps or hills in the backwoods of the world. They would do what we would do if we had some crews of astronauts investigating some distant planet. Our astronauts would have been given some detailed orders, such as go and make a flypast, take photos, films and make visual observations. Test for radioactivity, air oxygen content etc. Radio and teletype all your findings back to earth and then return home. Even more conceivable would be that orders would be given for them to land, if they found conditions "bearable", and especially if they had the technology (which UFO's obviously have) and investigate everything in sight and take soil and rock samples; if you find "beings" talk with them, film them and perhaps even kidnap one.

Now let us look at how the flying saucer people have behaved:

Technologically they are certainly very advanced, move at tremendous speeds, change direction at will, (often denying every known law of motion or gravity. They can seemingly appear and disappear from human vision or radarscreens with great ease. Theoretically and also practically they could land, take samples, kidnap people and leave for home, and almost unimpeded! So we must assume the obvious. These UFO's from other planets, (and on purely a mathematical probability there are habitants on other planets), have come, have seen, have sampled and returned home. Why would any representatives of any civilization advanced enough to come the tremendous distances involved, just play cat and mouse with a few hillbillies in Mississippi? The answer is self evident, they just would not bother with such a farce and over a period of 30 years!

So there has to be an equally simple answer to why UFO's behave the way they do. They have to be either from earth itself which can only explain their lack of curiosity and also accounts for their linguistic skills. Reinhold Schmidt states the crews of the flying saucer he flew with, spoke German, and those Adamski and others met, spoke English. They apparently looked like us and pretty well behaved as we do — undoubtedly because they are "from us".

Now it is not inconceivable that in the never-ending stream of time our race has either gone from here "out there" or we have been landed here or stranded here from "out there" eons of time ago. Legends and sagas of old can supply many pointers.

Could it mean that the German nation is indeed a colony, either from the German-speaking "Saturnians" with whom Reinhold Schmidt conversed or are they the outer-earth beach head of the inner-earth civilization previously mentioned? Is this perhaps the answer to the vexing question of why the Germans are "different"? Is this the explanation for their superb performance and genius as soldiers? Are they leading the world in precision engineering and in technology because they have dwelling amongst them a disproportionate number of "Saturnians" or "Atlantians"? Could this be the reason why they always rise stronger and Phoenix-like from the ashes of defeat? Was Hitler planted on this planet earth to pull back Western civilization from the brink of degenerate self-extinction — peacefully, if at all possible — through war, if necessary?

Should the above question be answered in the affirmative, then "The Last Battalion", when the time is ripe, will spring into action. With racial strife and economic disaster looming, how far away can "Der Tag" actually be? And finally, will the "Saucer Nazis", as a last resort, invade strategic areas militarily?

Members of "The Last Battalion" are already amongst us as soldiers, labourers, teachers, students, scientists — in fact, in all walks of life. Male and female, young and old. So look at your neighbours and your friends — how many of them do you think belong to "The Last Battalion"? Time will tell!

Eyewitnesses reports! All contain many elements of the Nazi-Saucer designs, technology similar as well as behaviour and flight patterns.

AF BANS PHOTO RELEASE

The Air Force last night banned publication of a photograph of an unidentified flying object seen over Ohio by hundreds of persons and chased 86 miles by police.

Police Chief Gerald Buchert, of Mantua, Ohio, about 25 miles east of Cleveland, said he photographed the object from the front lawn of his home.

Buchert, according to an Associated Press dispatch, said the Air Force told him not to release the photograph or permit pictures to be taken of it. He said the object looked like "two table saucers put together."

An East Palestine, Ohio, police officer and Portage County Sheriff's Deputy W. L. Neff said they "played tag" with the mysterious object for 86 miles through eastern Ohio before losing it near Conway, Pa.

PHOTOGRAPHED UFO—Mantua, O., Police Chief Gerald Bucher, left, gives information on unidentified flying object to Deputy Sheriff Dale Spaur, center, and radioman Robert Wilson after Bucher and several other police officers chased the object 85 miles from Mantua to Freedom, Pa. During the chase Bucher photographed the UFO. The photographs will not be released until viewed by federal authorities.

Flame-Shooting Phantom Plane

Airline Pilots See Wingless 2-Decker

ATLANTA, July 24.— (AP)—Two Eastern Airline pilots said they met a wingless two deck plane early today southwest of Montgomery, Ala. They said the strange ship shooting red flames and with a blue glow underneath the fuselage, passed the E. A. L. plane at their strange experience. Captain Childs said that they first sighted the object up ahead when nearing Montgomery.

"It was in line almost with our flight," he said. "We veered off to the left and the object turned to its left. When it came nearer to us, within better sight, its fuselage appeared to be about 100 feet in length and about four times the circumference of a B-29 fuselage.

2 ROWS OF WINDOWS

"It had two rows of windows, an upper and a lower. They were

SEEN AT 2:45 A. M.

The two pilots—Captain C. S. Childs, and co-pilot J. B. Whitted—were flying the Houston-to-Atlanta-to-Boston run. They left Houston, Tex., at 8:30 p. m. last night. This morning at 2:45 o'clock, 20 miles south of Montgomery they sighted the strange ship. After reaching Atlanta at 2:49

square. Out of the rear of the ship red flames were shooting 25 to 50 feet. There was a blue glow underneath the fuselage. The ship appeared to be doing between 500 and 700 miles an hour, heading toward New Orleans.

"Of the 20 passengers on board Childs said only one was awake and saw the other ship. He gave this passenger's name as C. L. McKelvie, Henelton Pike, Columbus, Ohio.

The E. A. L. ship went on from Atlanta to Boston today on its regular run.

At Montgomery, Maxwell and Dannelly army fields said they knew nothing about the report.

blue glow underneath the fuse- a. m. EST, the two pilots told of their strange experience. Captain Childs said that they first sighted the object up ahead when nearing Montgomery.

The pilots said the stranger looked like a "Buck Rogers rocket ship."

Radar Tracks Zipping Objects Near Air Base
8-2-65

OKLAHOMA CITY (UPI)—Air Force radar tracked four unidentified flying objects zipping along in a diamond formation at high altitude in a 50-mile radius of the sprawling Tinker Air Force Base Sunday night, authorities said.

At least eight law enforcement officers spotted the objects during the two hours immediately after the first sighting report which came just before sundown.

The sightings followed by less than 48 hours a Wynnewood, Okla., policeman's report of a UFO that emitted red, white and blue light near Wynnewood. The object was tracked on two radar screens early Saturday before it disappeared and then reappeared about 29 miles south of Tinker Base, officers said.

Wynnewood is about 29 miles south of Purcell, where the UFO's first were sighted Sunday night.

The Oklahoma Highway Patrol said a security officer at Tinker informed the patrol that the base's radar picked up from one to four UFO's at various times during the evening.

The objects were moving erratically, at an altitude of about 22,000 feet, the patrol quoted the officer as saying.

A base spokesman later would neither confirm nor deny that radar had tracked the objects. He said only that the Air Force would investigate the UFO reports.

U.F.O. reports from around the world and from pretty well-known people

THE THING ON THE BEACH

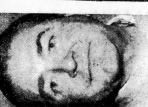

Sketch annotations:
- CONE. SILVERY GREY
- GRASS
- BLUEISH GREEN GLOW (ON RIM ONLY)
- LOWER CONE DARK GREY
- ALSO LEGS
- Leg Shadow?
- This leg? not very definite.
- NOTE: No PORT HOLES, Windows as such, or exterior antennae zere.

GLOWING IMPRESSION

THE SKETCH by Mr. Denis Crowe of the object he saw on Monday night on Vaucluse Beach. He described the saucer shape as silvery grey on top and darker grey beneath with a bluish-green glow at the rim and what might have been three or four "legs."

A green, glowing object that took off at high speed from a Vaucluse beach on Monday night in no way resembled conventional aircraft, Mr. Denis Crowe said last night.

Mr. Denis Crowe

in Coolong Road, Vaucluse, a Daily Telegraph reporter last night:

"It took off with a noise like an air forcibly released from a balloon.

"The noise was quite unlike any made by jet engines. Crowe said that the object, a giant disc, was bathed in a glow.

"He saw no sign of movement within the craft or any portholes or doors.

He said he became aware about 5.30 p.m. on Monday of a glow coming from the beach.

He went to investigate and saw that the glow emanated from a huge disc resting on the beach.

Near disc at take-off

He was within 50 or 60 feet of the disc when it took off.

"Its diameter appeared to be about 20 feet," he said.

"I estimate its height at nine feet, including what appeared to be legs protruding from the bottom.

"Its rim was glowing a greenish blue, while the top and bottom halves were dullish silver-grey.

"A hollow in the top could have been a glass dome."

Mr. Crowe said that as the object took off, a yellow or orange glow appeared beneath.

After a take-off run of only 50 or 60 feet, the craft climbed rapidly in the direction of Manly.

"I looked around, hoping to see someone else who saw what I saw, but

"After it took off, they were all strangely silent."

Mr. Denis Crowe

Mr. Crowe said that when he returned home he sat down to collect his thoughts.

He had dinner, then wrote down what was still vividly in his memory, and sketched the object as he recalled it.

The sketch is reproduced above.

[Mr. Crowe, an Englishman who has been in Australia for more than four years, was formerly a technical and illustrative artist with British aircraft companies.]

"At first I wondered whether I should say anything about what I had seen," he said.

"The natural reaction of most people might label me a crackpot.

"But I could not keep silent.

"I felt I had a moral obligation to speak of what I had seen."

UFO Is Reported In Western Area

ARKANSAS GAZETTE, Thurs., Aug. 12, 1965.

SANTA ANA, Cal. (A)—An unidentified flying object described as round, bright and with a long orange tail was seen by scores of Southern California residents Tuesday night and by at least three airline pilots flying over Arizona's Grand Canyon.

Viewers said the object moved rapidly from west to east in about 10 to 20 seconds. It appeared to descend rapidly, they said, then it would level and disappear to the east.

Three pilots reports a similar sighting and described it as a "large ball of fire with a tail, traveling west to east."

Similar reports came in from airports at China Lake, Palmdale, and Edwards Air Force Base, Cal., and the Albuquerque, N. M., Air Route Traffic Control Center.

Paper unknown Feb. 21 1956

Huge Flying Saucer Reported Over Paris

Paris —(U.P.)— The French government sought today to solve the mystery of the "phantom of Orly" a gigantic flying-saucer-like object which whirled across the airport's radar screen at supersonic speed last Friday.

It was the third time in less than a year that the "phantom" has been charted on radarscopes at the busy international airfield outside of Paris. The object was described as about twice the size of the largest known plane, moved at times at an estimated 2,000 miles an hour, and hovered around the airport for about four hours.

Mystery Object Over Hawaii

HONOLULU (UPI)—An unidentified flying object, traveling west at a "very high altitude and a high rate of speed," was sighted by hundreds of persons in the Hawaiian islands.

Two Air National Guard pilots said they saw the object north of the island of Kauai during a routine training mission in jet fighters at an altitude of 40,000 feet. Honolulu newspapers and radio stations were flooded with calls.

Capt. Jon Parish said he thought the object was "possibly a rocket or some sort of space object flying a predetermined course." Lt. George Joy said he thought it was the Milky Way at first, but then noticed that it left a visible vapor trail.

Witnesses in Honolulu said the object looked like a crescent-shaped moon falling into the sea. They said it was bright, and some said it appeared to be on fire.

ALASKAN TELLS OF MYSTERIOUS STREAK IN SKY

KETCHIKAN, April 15.—(AP) — A mysterious reddish orange streak across the sky over Annette Island was reported to the coast guard at 2 a. m. today.

Earl Leding said he sighted what seemed to be a flaming object hurtling westward at tremendous speed as he was returning by boat from Metlakatla, the Annette Island native community.

He said he and Ray Haldane saw the streak for about 40 seconds before it disappeared.

150

Navy Radar Spots Mystery Objects

WASHINGTON, Jan. 5 (AP). — The Air Force is investigating the reported sighting of two high-speed unidentified flying objects by Navy radar operators at Patuxent Naval Air Station, Md.

The Navy said Tuesday that the operators observed "two objects on their scope approaching at approximately 4800 miles an hour from 30 to 40 miles south" of the base at 8:30 P. M. Dec. 29.

The objects approached the naval air station, executed a tight turn and disappeared from the scope, the Navy said.

About the fastest aircraft in existence is the X-15 experimental plane, which has flown at 4104 miles an hour. The X-15 is based on the West Coast. It has a very short range.

7/8/65

See 'UFO'

BUENOS AIRES (UPI) — Argentine sailors at two Antarctic outposts saw a multi-colored "unidentified flying object" dawdling across the sky Saturday, the Navy Department announced Wednesday night.

"The object was discus-shaped and predominantly red and green in color, with occasional flashes of yellow, blue, orange and white. . ." The Navy announcement said.

"It was moving generally eastward, but at times it went west . . . at some moments, it appeared to hover . . .

"It was in view for 15 to 20 minutes, allowing ample time to photograph it . . . (the object) was seen by members of the naval detachments at Deception and Orcadas."

Eerie Object Seen Over Antarctica '65

BUENOS AIRES, July 7. — (Reuters) — Argentines at two Antarctic bases have confirmed reports by British and Chilean scientists of the appearance four days ago of an unusual celestial body over the frozen subcontinent.

The object, observed and photographed by the Argentine Navy men last Saturday night, was shaped like a double-convex lens. It was colored mainly red and green, a Navy statement said.

The object made no noise, and moved generally eastward at changing speeds before disappearing.

An earlier report from a British Antarctic base said the object made geomagnetic instruments wild.

Ten-Gallon UFO Sighted at Sault

SAULT STE. MARIE, Ont. (CP) — An unidentified flying object shaped like a "ten-gallon hat" was sighted here Friday night.

Darlene Wagner, 15, said she saw the object about 10:20 p.m., silently descending to the top of an oil storage tank across the road from her home. It landed on the oil tank.

The girl said the object was shaped like a hat, the crown glowing red, the brim blue. There were flashing blue and white lights at each edge of the "brim."

London Free Press
May 6, 1966

151

Object Filmed By X15 Still Big Mystery

Aug. 9, 1962

Aug. 9, 1962

EDWARDS AIR FORCE BASE, CALIF. (UPI)—A possibility the X15 encountered strange phenomena in space arose Thursday with scientists unable to identify a mysterious object both sighted and photographed by Maj. Bob White on a soaring flight by the rocket ship.

Scientists said Wednesday they could give no explanation whatsoever for the objects that appeared near the X15 on July 17 when White skyrocketed to a world airplane altitude record of nearly 60 miles.

"It is impossible to explain the object's presence at this time," space agency scientists said.

The National Aeronautics and Space Administration, after intensively studying White's sighting report and films from a tail movie camera, on the X15, released photographs of an object that darted above and behind the plane.

The photographs, taken from the movie films, show an object that looks like a fluttering piece of paper and which scientists describe as being "grey-white."

White, from his cockpit near the nose of the rocket ship, reported seeing what looked to him like a piece of paper the size of his hand "going along with the ship" at an altitude of 270,000 feet—over 50 miles high.

Pilots Tell Of Saucers Flying In Formation

MIAMI, July 16. —(UP)— Two veteran air-line pilots added to the flying-saucer lore today accounts of seeing eight huge discs zipping in formation at supersonic speed near Norfolk, Va.

W. B. Nash, 35, and W. H. Fortenberry, 30, pilots of Pan American Airways, said the "glowing, orange-red" saucers maneuvered too sharply for human endurance at a speed of "far above 1,000 miles per hour."

"Whoever was in those things," the pilots declared, "had capabilities far beyond our own. Those things absolutely did not contain any human being as we know them."

Nash and Fortenberry said they were flying their DC-4 with ten company officials aboard southward between Newport News, Va., and Norfolk Monday night when the saucers appeared 6,000 feet below them, at about 2,000 feet altitude.

Mystery object

SANTA MARIA, Azores (UPI) — An airport spokesman Saturday said a mysterious flying object apparently stopped all electro-magnetic watches at the Santa Maria Airport when it flew slowly over this island Friday. He said a white cylindrical object was seen flying northwest at an altitude of 33,000 feet and attempts to identify it were unsuccessful.

THE AUGUSTA
CHRONICLE-HERALD
SUNDAY, JULY 11, 1965

Pilot believes he saw manned space-ship

THE pilot of a Pan-American airliner, flying almost four miles up between New York and Paris, this morning, reported that he sighted what he believed was a space ship with people on board.

In a brief message from the clipper, Captain J. Cone, said it was visible for only 30 seconds and that the object had vertical tail fins. It was travelling very fast in a south-westerly direction between the stars, Elnath and Castor.

The message was flashed to a U.S. coastguard cutter.

There were 119 people including 12 crew members on board the jet liner, which later landed at Paris. It was flying at an altitude of 20,000 feet when the object was sighted.

Gave position

Other brief details given in the message gave the object's position as 53.40 degrees north, 58 degrees west, which would be slightly north-east of Goose Bay, Newfoundland, about 2,000 miles west of Ireland.

The report has set off speculation in international circles studying space aeronautics, the dominant view being that it was a secret Russian attempt to send men to outer space, probably to the moon.

It is expected that a report will be sent to the United States Government for investigation.

On DEW line

The object was sighted almost on the D.E.W. line, the distant early warning radar screen which protects the entire north-west coast of America and Canada from attack.

Mystery Object Buzzes Planes

TOKYO, March 21 (Reuters). —Two Japanese civilian pilots reported ' their planes were buzzed Thursday by an unidentified flying object, an air safety officer in southwestern Japan said Sunday.

A spokesman for the Air Safety office at Takamatsu on Shikoku Island said the planes were a Convair 240 airliner and a private Piper Apache plane.

The newspaper Mainichi Shimbun quoted the airliner pilot as saying an object about 15 yards in diameter and radiating a greenish luminescence approached the plane at about 20 miles an hour, wheeled abruptly and flew alongside for about three minutes before making off.

THE PHILADELPHIA INQUIRER.

Dublin Evening Press

September 23rd 1959

153

PAPER UNKNOWN   Dec. 4, 1965

Unidentified Objects Sighted by Astronauts

SPACE CENTER. Houston. Tex.. Dec 4 (AP).—Twice in the early part of their space flight, astronauts Frank Borman and James Lovell reported seeing objects that were not explained immediately. On the second orbit. Borman said. "We have a bogey at 10 o'clock high."

There was some static in the transmission and the space center had to ask three times for explanation. Borman said they could see the spacecraft booster "as a brilliant body against the sun," slowly tumbling and that three of four miles ahead of the spacecraft there were "what looks like hundreds of little particles."

In addition, he said, there was the "bogey." That's an airman's term for another object.

On the third revolution, while burning fuel to raise the orbit. Lovell reported "we hit something."

Space Center: "You hit something during the burn?"

Lovell: "Something came forward by the right window. Look-

Nov. 19. 1953

British Radar Tracks Air 'Object'

LONDON, Nov. 19.—(AP)—An object described by observers as huge and glowing and probably metallic has been tracked by radar high over England twice this month, the War Office disclosed last night.

Official reports of the sightings have been made by members of two army radar crews. They estimated that the object's altitude was 60,000 feet.

The reports were on November 3. The first report said the object was kept in sight from 2:30 to 3:10 p. m. A similar report was made that day by two flying officers of the Royal Air Force. They were at 20,000 feet in a jet plane, they said, when the object passed far overhead at "tremendous speed."

They're Up There Again

Bangor, Maine, March 24, (UPI)—A Bangor man said today he fired four shots at a glowing, cigar-shaped unidentified flying object late last night and believes he hit it with at least one bullet.

John King, 22, said the craft responded by zooming skyward, almost straight up, and swiftly vanished to the North. He said he thought he saw a similar object some distance away moments later.

Report Flying Object In Alexandria Area

ALEXANDRIA (AP) — Three state policemen and several other persons reported they saw an unidentified flying object about 30 miles south of here last night.

Troopers P. E. Lemoine and H. J. Roy said the object "definitely was not a plane" and described it as

N.Y. NEWS MARCH 25, 1966

154

UFOs Spotted In Minnesota

MINNEAPOLIS (A) — Unidentified Flying Objects were spotted over parts of Minnesota and North Dakota Monday night.

Dozens of police officers on patrol between 12:20 and 2:30 a. m. reported sightings in the Minneapolis-St. Paul area. According to various reports, the objects "bobbed, dipped, hovered, stopped, jerked along and sped away."

An officer in suburban Shorewood radioed his dispatcher: "Boys, I hope you don't think I'm crazy, but I just got passed by a star."

The airport control tower said it had seen nothing on radar. The tower said also that a number of B-52 military aircraft were in the area.

Sky Object Tracked by AFB Radar

OKLAHOMA CITY (P) — Tinker Air Force Base officials reported tracking an unidentified flying object by radar early Saturday before it suddenly disappeared.

The object was first sighted by Lewis Sikes, a Wynnewood policeman. He said it appeared to emit a red, blue and white light.

The Highway Patrol told Tinker authorities of the sighting and Tinker picked up the object on radar. Carswell Air Force Base at Fort Worth, Tex., also located the object on radar.

The object was ' to a location 29 miles Tinker before it disapp...

Officials at Tinker ... no air-

Tulsa Daily World, Sunday, August 1, 1965.

'Saucers' Fly Beside Plane

DETROIT — (P) — The pilot of an American Airlines DC-6 passenger plane said Wednesday three mysterious objects that looked like shining saucers appeared to accompany the plane for 45 minutes last night on its nonstop flight from Newark, N. J., to Detroit.

Capt. Peter Killian of Syosset, N. Y., who has flown passenger planes for 15 years, said "I have never seen anything like it before."

Killian said other members of the crew and the 35 passengers also saw the flying objects. The plane left Newark at 7:10 p.m.

* * *

KILLIAN and co-pilot John Dee of Nyack, N. Y., said they lost the three strange objects in the haze when they started their descent for landing at Detroit's Metropolitan Airport while the plane was over Cleveland, Ohio.

The three bright whitish lights first were sighted while the plane was flying at 8,500 feet between Philipsburg and Bradford, Pa.

Mysterious Object Seen

HELSINKI (UPI) — Mysterious ball and cigar - shaped

155

as EVENING CHRONICLE
7/4/57

'Flying object' near Russia

A flying object was seen over northern Finland near the Russian border, say Press reports in Helsinki.

One report said that the object was seen near Kuusamo, about 20 miles from the border.

ENGLAND

Air-Line Pilot Sees Mysterious Flying Objects

CHICAGO, July 18. — (UP) — A veteran air-line pilot reported seeing four flying objects moving at high speed over Denver last night.

Capt. Paul L. Carpenter of American Airlines said he and his crew spotted the objects after a flight ahead of them radioed them to be on the look-out.

Carpenter said the objects looked like planets and had a yellowish tinge. He said he saw one by itself, then two others and finally a fourth. He estimated their altitude at 25,000 to 30,000 feet and said he thought they were traveling at about 3,000 miles an hour.

UFO Watch Ordered

MEXICO CITY (A)—The airport commander here, Luis Angel Jara Monroy, has ordered control tower men to keep watch for flying saucers. Public relations chief Ricardo de Zaldo said he had no doubt some strange objects were seen by the hundreds who phoned in one night but he doubted they were from other planets.

Did Hillary see Chinese rocket?

ENGLAND

KATMANDU, Thursday. — Sir Edmund Hillary, the New Zealand explorer, said today that he had seen "phenomena" across the Nepal-Tibet border in the Mount Everest region which could have been anything, including a Chinese rocket.

He said that while camping in a glacier in October members of his Himalayan expedition saw a streak of vapour trail and a flash of fire moving in a zig-zag.—Reuter.

down branch by branch."

The boy, Raymond Grant, was taken home, suffering from shock.

ENGLAND

Flying saucer 'hisses'

Men on the tarmac at London Airport were certain last night that they saw a flying saucer. One described it—" white, with a blue flame from its tail. Speed about 600 miles an hour, and it hissed."

Mr Fred Perrior, airport porter, said it was a foot long and six inches wide, and it kept a straight course.

But control tower officials neither saw it nor heard the hiss.

THE PEOPLE 18/8/5

I've seen flying saucer—Priest

ENGLAND

AN Anglican missionary reported to his headquarters yesterday: "I've seen a flying saucer with men inside it.

"The men waved and exchanged signals with us," said Father W. B. Gill, of Boiana Anglican Mission, Papua, in a report which reached Brisbane yesterday.

156

Radar Crews Get Solid Fix on UFOs

HOUGHTON (Mich.)—(UPI)—Personnel at the U.S. Air Force radar base in the Keweenan Peninsula yesterday reported "solid radar contact" with seven to 10 unidentified flying objects moving in a "V" formation over Lake Superior.

The objects were moving out of the southwest and were heading north - northeast at about 9,000 miles per hour, the men said. They were 5,200 to 17,000 feet high.

One of the men at the base said three other radar stations, in North Dakota, Minnesota and Luther Air Station in Canada, also reported spotting the objects. He said another station reported electronic jamming of its radar.

Seven other objects were spotted over Duluth and jet interceptors gave chase, he said, but they could not maintain the speed of the UFO's and were easily outdistanced.

The radar personnel, Air Force enlisted men, asked that their names not be disclosed.

2 SOUTH AFRICAN POLICEMEN REPORT SIGHTING OF 'SAUCER'

JOHANNESBURG, South Africa—South African police and scientists investigated Thursday a report that a flying saucer-type object had landed on a main highway near Pretoria, the country's administrative capital.

Two patrolling police officers reported seeing the flaming "saucer," about 30 feet in diameter, shortly after midnight. One of them, Koos de Klerk, said that the shiny copper-colored object resembled a giant spinning top.

The two men claimed that, as they approached the object, it took off silently at great speed with flames shooting out of its underside.

Scientists who examined the spot where the officers said that they saw the object are reported to have found that a six-foot wide section of the tarred road had been badly burned. Grass on either side of the highway also was reported slightly scorched.

(Associated Press)

THE BOSTON HERALD, FRIDAY, SEPT. 17, 1965

In Conquest of Cosmos

Earthlings, Planet Men To Join Forces, Red Says

London, Sept. 29 (AP).—A Russian scientist predicted today that space-probing earthlings eventually would meet up with beings from other worlds.

And together they would go on to conquer the cosmos.

"Soviet science already commands the means to send cosmic rockets to Mars and Venus," claimed Moscow radio.

To be sure of getting to Venus a rocket will have to be set off precisely at 11.5 kilometers (7.46 miles) per second —"somewhat greater" than the speed of Russia's rocket which hit the moon, the broadcast said.

In man's conquest of the cosmos, Moscow radio reported, astronomer Feliks Segal believes the space travelers first will colonize the moon. Then they will conquer the rest of the planets. Finally they will venture forth into other solar systems.

In a broadcast beamed to North America, Moscow radio said the moon at present was no place for man to make a home. It has no atmosphere and man could not breathe there. Daytime temperatures rise to 130 degrees centigrade but the nights are unbearably cold, the thermometer dropping to minus 160 degrees.

Moscow radio said one Russian scientist estimates that one inhabited planetary system must exist for every million stars.

"Consequently there must be about 150,000 inhabited planetary systems in our galaxy.

"On some of them life exists in lower forms. But there must be planets, too whose inhabitants may even be higher than man in point of development.

"Some of them may even have begun to make flights into space. Therefore we should have meetings with them.

"If such meetings do take place, they may result in the co-ordination of the efforts of man and these other intelligent beings in the great work of combating the elemental forces of nature."

Strange Air Object Seen In N.M.

ALAMOGORDO, N.M. (UPI)—A cigar-shaped unidentified flying object was reported seen Friday night near the place where the "manhigh" Air Force space balloon landed Wednesday.

The object was reported by John Romero, identified as a missile engineer, on the White Sands Proving Ground. But he said it had a fan-shaped tail and four pin-point spots of lights on the side like portholes.

THE NEWARK STAR-LEDGER, FRIDAY, FEBRUARY 20, 1959

Says 'saucers' seen in Far North

By JOHN LESTER
Staff Writer

Unidentified Flying Objects, more commonly known as Flying Saucers, again have been seen "maneuvering and landing" in Northern Alaska and the North Pole area, UFO authority Lee R. Munsick of Morristown told members of the Denville Rotary Club yesterday.

Speaking at a luncheon meeting at the Rockaway River Country Club, Munsick, formerly assistant director of the National Investigations Committee on Aerial Phenomena, told Rotarians

these most recent sightings in the Frozen North took place within the past two weeks, "as nearly as can be determined at this time."

The Alaskan sighting involved a single disc-type craft that was seen by a small party of trappers about 200 miles east of Umiat, Munsick said.

The men estimated the UFO was about two miles away when they first noticed it, Munsick reported, that it rose and descended to within a few feet of the ground several times, then flew slowly

in a tight circle before disappearing.

They described it as "red colored."

Munsick attributed this to the fact that there are numerous instances on record of UFOs' glowing when in motion, a deep orange at low speeds, nearly white at high speeds.

The Polar sighting was made by two Norwegian soldiers, although no further details are available.

The Norwegian embassy, Munsick said, claimed to have no record of this sighting but added

that all information on UFOs and their sightings were considered classified.

This latest North Pole sighting is at least the fourth in which members of the Norwegian military have figured as far as is known, the speaker said.

In September, 1955, he recalled, a representative of the Norwegian Gneral Staff revealed that "special details" assigned to observe the Arctic region "are now convinced" it was being used as a base by UFOs, especially during bad weather "when we are forced back to our bases."